BREA IN BREATHE OUT

INHALE ENERGY
AND EXHALE STRESS
BY GUIDING AND CONTROLLING
YOUR BREATHING

James E. Loehr, Ed.D. and Jeffrey A. Migdow, M.D.
Produced by Jerome Agel

TIME
LIFE
BOOKS

ALEXANDRIA, VIRGINIA

Simple as these exercises may seem (and they are), before embarking on any exercise program, you should consult with your medical doctor.

To Mike, Pat, and Jeff—my breath of life.
—JIM

To my parents, Ben and Eloise, who breathed life into me,
and my daughter, Kelly, who is always a breath of fresh air.
—JEFF

We also wish to thank everyone whose breathing floats through these pages:
Fred Lazarus's, Marion D. S. Dreyfus's, and Jerry Agel's—
especially Jerry's, without which and whom . . .
—JIM/JEFF

TIME® LIFE BOOKS

Time-Life Books is a division of Time Life Inc.

TIME LIFE INC.
President and CEO: George Artandi

TIME-LIFE CUSTOM PUBLISHING
Vice President and Publisher: Terry Newell
Vice President of Sales and Marketing: Neil Levin
Director of Acquisitions and Editorial Resources: Jennifer Pearce
Editor for Special Markets: Anna Marlis Burgard

Cover Design: Anna Marlis Burgard
Design Production: Universal Communications

Library of Congress Cataloging-in-Publication Data
Loehr, James E.
    [Take a deep breath]
    Breathe in, breathe out: inhale energy and exhale stress by guiding and controlling your
    breathing/James E. Loehr and Jeffrey A. Migdow; produced by Jerome Agel.
        p.   cm.
    Previously published: New York: Villard Books, 1986.
    ISBN 0-7370-1611-6 (softcover:alk. paper)
    1. Breathing exercises. 2. Stress management. I. Migdow, Jeffrey A. II. Title.
    RA782.L64 1999
    613'.192--dc21   99-38896   CIP

TABLE OF CONTENTS

Breathing Can Save Your Life

When you breathe, the quality of the air you breathe is all-important in terms of your health and vitality.

The key factor is the quality of the molecular air you bring into and through your lungs.

You want to inhale air that is oxygenated as much as possible. You want to breathe in air that has little, if any, carbon monoxide or other toxins, such as ammonia, benzine, and formaldehyde, or pollutants that originate in industrial pollution and automobile pollution, among sundry commercial sources.

There also are toxins in the chemical makeup of carpeting and paints. There are molds in every home.

As we all know, air pollution has been a huge, huge problem in the last 30 to 40 years. People in many of our principal cities, such as Los Angeles, New York, and Chicago, have been advised to remain indoors on many summer days, especially if they are elderly or have a cardiac or a respiratory illness. Pollution in Tokyo has been life-threatening; people have to walk around with face masks because of the high incidence of toxins in the everyday air.

Not too long ago, automobile exhaust threatened to overwhelm us with carbon monoxide. Carbon monoxide binds the hemoglobin in our red blood cells 30 times faster than oxygen does. When oxygen intake falters, your principal energy source falters, or is lost.

Pollutants affect your nervous system by reducing its ability to work effectively. Pollutants overstress your liver and your kidneys, organs of detoxification.

Congress woke up in 1970. It legislated the Clean Air Act, because it was convinced that air pollution indeed aggravates health problems such as asthma, heart disease, and bronchitis. Industries and gasoline makers were forced to clean up their processes.

In the Clean Air Act, Congress found that the predominant part of the Nation's population was located in rapidly expanding metropolitan and other urban areas, which generally cross the boundary lines of local jurisdictions and often extend into two or more States.

It also found that the growth in the amount and complexity of air pollution brought about by urbanization, industrial development, and the increasing use of motor vehicles resulted in mounting dangers to the public health and welfare, including injury to agricultural crops and livestock, damage to, and the deterioration of, property, and hazards to air and ground transportation.

Also, it decided that air-pollution prevention (that is, the reduction or elimination, through any measures, of the amount of pollutants produced or created at the source) and air-pollution control at its source should be the primary responsibility of State and local governments.

Federal financial assistance and leadership were essential for the development of cooperative Federal, State, regional, and local programs to prevent and control air pollution.

The Congressional Act sought:

—to protect and enhance the quality of the Nation's air resources so as to promote the public health and welfare and the productive capacity of its population;

—to initiate and accelerate a national research and development program to achieve the prevention and control of air pollution;

—to provide technical and financial assistance to State and local governments in connection with the development and execution of their air-pollution prevention and control programs; and

—to encourage and assist the development and operation of regional air-pollution prevention and control programs.

When future president Ronald W. Reagan was governor of California, he declared that if he were to single out the one major issue that most likely would dominate the political attention of the United States in the 1970s, it would be environmental protection. "What good is a booming economy," Governor Reagan asked, "if the air is too foul to breathe, the water too polluted to drink, and our cities too cluttered with ugly examples of environmental neglect to provide comfortable living?"

Since Congress legislated the Clean Air Act, each state has had primary responsibility for ensuring air quality within its borders. Emissions of all airborne microscopic particles under 10 microns in diameter have had to be reduced. (A human hair, for comparison, is 100 microns in diameter.)

In 1990, House and Senate negotiators settled years of regional disputes. Congress strengthened and broadened the Government's authority: Stricter standards were set; timetables for cutting chemical contamination sharply were established. Production of chemicals that destroy the ozone layer was to cease.

Yes, the quality of our air has improved dramatically, thanks to cleaner cars, cleaner power plants, and cleaner fuels.

Unfortunately, the indoors air we breathe is less healthy than it was three decades ago. For instance, most carpeting today is the product of synthetic chemicals rather than natural substances; those chemicals flood your home for at least a year after the carpet is put down.

House paints have more chemicals today than they did. Those chemicals seem to float around, envelop us, for eons.

Insulation materials present problems. Insulation saves on energy costs, but it keeps air from moving in your home.

There was lots of air in log cabins. The log cabin breathed. It was like a huge lung. To a very great degree, moving air prevents molds and funguses and other microorganisms from growing.

Research discovered that dwellings have dead-air spaces, where air moves hardly at all, if at all. Toxins from carpeting and paints and other sources build up in those spaces. The carbon dioxide that you and your family and your guests exhale builds up. The carbon dioxide in the stagnant air binds with the body's hemoglobin. Alas, your blood cells have little ability to make energy that's needed.

Many homes today have a sick environment. Behind walls and under floors is a tremendous amount of mold and chemicals. Yes, people become sick, sometimes very sick, simply breathing at home.

Every month, Dr. Migdow sees new patients whose symptoms clearly are brought on by a sick-home environment.

Our advice: Open your windows. Let fresh air pour through. Breathing can empower your life.

—James E. Loehr, Ed.D.
—Jeffrey A. Migdow, M.D.
June, 1999

TEST YOUR BREATHING POWER

n the chapters that follow, you will read that psychology and modern medicine have advanced knowledge of the ways in which breathing interacts with the body and the mind; that Nature intended us to breathe like newborn babies; that without regular, babylike deep breathing, stale air stagnates in the lower portion of the lungs, stifling energy and spirit; that a ragged breathing pattern is associated with risk of heart disease; that breath may be the most convenient way to ease childbirth and to combat emotional reaction to stress; that breathing breaks are an ideal, no-sweat adjunct to a corporate fitness policy; that breathing unequally or alternately through the nostrils can build energy, induce relaxation, heighten awareness, even access creativity; that breathing techniques can manipulate hemispheric brain dominance...You *can* breathe new life into yourself!

True or false: When breath is adjusted, improved, directed:

	True	False
1. Stress is reduced.	____	____
2. Weight may be shed.	____	____
3. Sleep becomes sounder.	____	____
4. Mood improves.	____	____
5. Allergies and asthma are alleviated.	____	____
6. Blood pressure is lowered.	____	____
7. Smoking is given up.	____	____
8. Sports performances are sharper.	____	____
9. Constipation and headaches are relieved.	____	____
10. Sinuses clear up.	____	____
11. Sex becomes even more enjoyable.	____	____
12. Appearance improves.	____	____
13. Work is more efficient, communication more effective.	____	____
14. Menstrual cramping is overcome.	____	____
15. Pollution is cleaned out.	____	____
16. Emotions are harnessed.	____	____
17. Harmony of body and mind is exalted, maximum potential is reached.	____	____

(*Answers appear on page 191.*)

CHAPTER ONE

BREATH IS LIFE

...sweet is the breath of morn...
—John Milton, *Paradise Lost*

Oxygen: the first and most basic necessity of life, the essential element of your moment-by-moment involvement with the air around you.

Life begins with your first breath. You will breathe in oxygen ten to sixteen or more times in the next minute. You will take about one hundred million breaths before you take your last.

But breathing is far more than inhaling air containing oxygen, circulating it in your body, consuming its benefits, and exhaling carbon dioxide. Philosophers and physicians have always recognized the basic relationship between breathing and life energy. For three thousand years, the philosophy of yoga has held that control of "vital breath" is the key to good physical health and to calm, clear thinking. In this century, science has advanced our understanding of how breathing interacts with the body and the mind. Research has shown that slowing down and deepening our breath shifts us from the stress response to the relaxation response; this slows the heart, normalizes blood pressure, increases blood flow to the digestive system, deepens sleep, increases energy, focus, concentration, and memory—optimal breathing not only helps prevent or cure disease, it raises performance levels in school and sports.

By combining the wisdom of the sages and the ages with recent medical discoveries, we have developed breathing techniques for attaining peak performance, managing stress, and improving overall health. They are easy to master—they become a part of you—they can have profound effects. A drastic change in lifestyle isn't even necessary to use breath to feel both stronger and more peaceful. Simply exercising the routines you need to, or those with which you feel most comfortable, can lead to a day changed for the oh-so-much-better.

What do we mean by the term *breathing technique?* We mean the conscious movement of breath to achieve a state of relaxed vitality so that optimum health is reached and maintained.

We mean the training of breath as a tool to achieve heightened energy and awareness.

We mean the application of breath to solve specific problems—lowering blood pressure, for example, or helping to stop smoking once and for all, or even helping to make waiting in lines less stressful.

The purpose of this book is *inspirational* in the literal sense: to breathe new life into oneself, to reintegrate body and mind.

Within you is a tremendous reserve of energy that can be channeled into a harmonious self. The reason it may be stifled is simple.

Normally, you inhale just enough air to get by, to keep your body at maintenance level. Although you feel perfectly all right, you aren't providing enough energy to gear up to maximum potential. What's more, the chances are you are not breathing deeply enough to remove toxins that build up through continual wear and tear on your cells; the battery runs down. Toxic load is a major reason you feel sluggish and unmotivated. Most people don't clean out the lower portion of their lungs. Stale air hangs around there.

Tension is the straitjacket that constricts your lungs, that keeps you from realizing your potential through breath. Tension creates a state of internal war that limits action.

Age compounds problems. As you grow older, you will lose more and more flexibility in your chest and lungs. If measures aren't taken to counteract this disposition, tightening becomes worse. You will hunch when you walk. You will live on edge. You will seem to run out of air. You will gulp, you will gasp.

Lamentable trends *can* be reversed. The means are available just about at will. Nature has provided you with the ability to take in *seven times* the amount of oxygen you normally inhale. The nature of Nature is designed to be taken advantage of.

Do it right now.

Take a deep, full breath.

Now, exhale it slowly. *Slowly.*

Do it again. Take another deep, full breath. Let it out slowly.

And again.

Establish a nice, quiet rhythm. Always exhale more slowly than you inhale.

Already you should feel calmer, more relaxed.

If you do nothing more than this simple exercise every time you become tense, your sense of well-being will begin to change for the better.

We want to tell you how breathing works to achieve life-giving effects, how it lets you be the best you. Here is *the* basic breathing technique:

ABDOMINAL BREATH: THE NATURAL BREATH

For maximum effect, do this exercise in a relaxed setting where you can be alone for at least a few minutes.

1. Lie on your back or stand or sit comfortably and place your hands on your stomach (abdomen). It is easier to lie on your back.
2. Inhale slowly and deeply, letting your abdomen expand like a balloon. (Keep a hand on your abdomen. You will feel it expanding.)
3. Let the abdomen fall as you exhale slowly; you are releasing old, stale air.
4. Inhale easily. Feel your abdomen expand again.
5. Press the air out as you contract, as you pull in your abdomen while exhaling.

You have now become reacquainted with the abdominal component of your breath. *Reacquainted?* Yes, because we were all born breathing abdominally, properly.

Look at a sleeping baby. Its little tummy moves outward easily and fully as it breathes in air. Its diaphragm—the sheetlike muscle between the lungs and the abdomen— contracts downward to let its lungs expand and fill with air. Simultaneously, its abdominal muscles relax; they don't fight movement. Air fills the *entire* lungs. The whole process is soothing, healthful.

The opposite of diaphragmatic, or abdominal, breathing is thoracic, or chest, breathing. In thoracic breathing the abdomen is never totally relaxed. The diaphragm does not enjoy the freedom to contract downward. As a result, the chest-breather must rely more and more on his middle- and upper-chest areas. Chest expansion can't by itself deliver

the same amount of air unless it is done in concert with abdominal action. Because of this inefficiency, the thoracic-
breather (a category that includes most adults) has to work
harder at his breathing. He must breathe more frequently:
at least sixteen times a minute, instead of ten to twelve efficient, relaxed abdominal inspirations. Think what a saving
of energy, what a saving of wear and tear on the lungs can
be realized by redeveloping the inborn, natural, efficient abdominal breath!

How is the easy rhythm, that perfect wave, lost in the
first place? Through tension.

In addition to being subject to modern life's manifold
stresses, one is constantly reminded to project an image em-
blematic of tension in the gut. Women conform to the
narrow-waisted, chesty image of movie stars. Few wear the
tight corsets that were popular in Victorian times, but they
tend to constrict their stomach in the belief a waist can't be
tiny enough. Men suck in their stomach and puff out their
chest so they can project a macho image. But constricting
the stomach merely fools oneself and, in the process, strait-
jackets breathing.

The first step in regaining optimal breath and its benefits
is to become aware of breathing patterns and the connection between the patterns and emotional states. Think how
you are breathing at this very moment. Think of the ways
you breathe during different activities of the day. Compare
and contrast how you breathe when you are washing dishes,
feeding the baby, feeling angry, taking a stroll, driving in
heavy traffic, making a sales call, watching television, typing the same letter to fifty people, reading. The less pleasant
the experience, the more likely it is that you breathe in a
shallow, thoracic, *constricting* pattern.

Researchers at the University of California have confirmed this breath correlation. Test subjects were shown two

films, one pleasant, the other unpleasant. Their reactions to the unpleasant film included thoracic breathing.

If the cumulative effects of unpleasant events continue unchecked, they repeatedly reinforce thoracic breathing. The pattern is eventually established as the norm. Reinforcement "happens."

In fact, many people hold their breath during stress. Breathholding is in itself stressful, aggravating mood and decreasing performance. With a little conscious effort, abdominal breathing can be effected.

Fuller development of the basic Abdominal Breath for relaxation is called, appropriately, the Relaxation Breath. Its goals are release of tension from specific parts of the body and overall relaxation. It can be done in any position that is comfortable, but not while moving.

THE RELAXATION BREATH

1. Do five to ten Abdominal Breaths.
2. Continue the Abdominal Breath as you imagine that with each inhalation you are breathing into a tense or a painful part of your body. (To locate tension accurately, you may need to do neck-rolls, shoulder-shrugs, leg-stretches, buttock-shifts, foot-shakes.)
3. Imagine, with each exhalation, tension streaming out of your nostrils; the ache you are concentrating on really begins to ease.
4. Continue the Abdominal Breath and imaging for a few minutes—or longer as needed.

When breathing for relaxation, it is best to employ a lengthy *exhalation*. *Ahhhhhhhhhh*. Most people find it helpful to breathe with a count. Begin with inhalations and exhalations of equal duration: in—one, two, three, four; out—one, two, three, four. Presently change to a count of four in and eight out. You will feel relaxed all over.

Centuries of contemplation by mediators all over the world have established ratios of breathing for a relaxed, aware state. The mind remains clear and the body rests.

As you read on, you will learn how directed breathing can be the cornerstone of a personal program of preventive medicine. In Chapter Three we launch a full frontal attack on stress, that bugaboo of modern life. Conquer stress and you're all but home free.

The power of breath is awesome. Many accomplished singers, musicians, dancers, and actors employ breathing techniques to perfect their art. Many truly incredible feats have been accomplished through harnessing the power of breath control. Houdini's amazing underwater survival stunts were possible only through a phenomenal understanding of the power of breath control—and, of course, knowing how to slip out of padlocked crates.

Natural, comfortable, primal, releasing, relaxing—these are the terms associated with proper breathing as one eases into it. Our techniques free up the breath. They help the entire system breathe in the way it must for best effects, for escape from the chains of unconscious mental conditioning and control. Breaking the blocks leads to harmony with activities and experiences.

The art of breathing—the most basic function of life—allows you to be alive in every moment, *naturally*. Breath *is* life!

CHAPTER TWO

WITH EVERY BREATH YOU TAKE: THE PHYSIOLOGY OF BREATHING

With every breath you take, you can look better, feel healthier, *be* healthier.

Your skin—your largest organ—is an organ of elimination, as are your two lungs. When you breathe optimally, you eliminate even more gaseous toxins through your lungs. There is less of a load on your skin, which takes on a healthier glow—from *within*. How you breathe indeed affects your whole being. In this chapter we shall give more examples of the Breath Connection.

THE LUNGS

Blood flow is greater in the lower part of the lungs because of gravity. When you are seated or standing at rest,

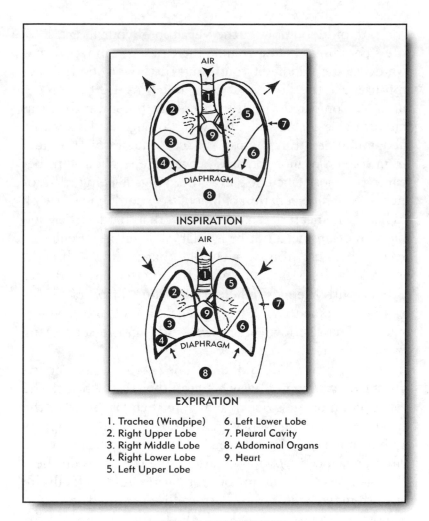

1. Trachea (Windpipe)   6. Left Lower Lobe
2. Right Upper Lobe   7. Pleural Cavity
3. Right Middle Lobe   8. Abdominal Organs
4. Right Lower Lobe   9. Heart
5. Left Upper Lobe

ANATOMY OF BREATHING

The diaphragm acts as a pump to change the size of the chest cavity. On inspiration, the diaphragm relaxes and moves downward, creating a vacuum. This vacuum draws the air into the lungs (top middle arrow). We can also consciously contract our internal intercostal muscles that pull the rib cage outward, increasing the vacuum, thus increasing the flow of air into the lungs. It is obvious that a strong, flexible diaphragm and flexible rib muscles are imperative for optimal breathing. On expiration, the diaphragm contracts up and causes the air in the lungs to be squeezed out. The external intercostal muscles between the ribs now contract and pull the rib cage and chest wall in, maximizing the release of air by the lungs. The movement of the diaphragm gives a gentle, constant massage to the heart and abdominal organs. (An interesting note is that the left lung contains two lobes while the right lung contains three. This evolutionary imbalance probably came about to compensate for the heart being placed more on the left side of the body.)

the rate of blood flow in the very top of your lungs is .07 liters per minute. Flow volume increases as it moves downward. At the middle of your lungs the flow is .66 liter per minute. At the bottom it is as much as 1.29 liters per minute. Compared with the upper part, the lower third has almost twice the flow of air flowing through it. This is why abdominal breathing helps to reduce one's respiratory rate from sixteen or more breaths per minute to about ten. Because the most efficient part of the lungs is being used for richer, easier oxygenation of blood, they don't have to work as hard. The heart doesn't have to work as hard, either, and blood pressure need not be as high. The entire circulatory system benefits from this simple change in the breath. There is far less wear and tear on the internal environment.

Even with the most efficient breathing, of course, lungs can never come to a full rest. Theirs is a miraculous performance. Here is how these hard-working, life-supporting organs function.

Lungs are two balloonlike organs nestled in the body's chest cavity. Pumping away between them is the heart. The lungs fill all of the space available to them, right up to the inside of the rib cage. They are enveloped in a thin, slippery lining called the visceral pleura. Coating the inside of the rib cage is a corresponding parietal pleura. Between these linings is a small amount of lubricating fluid to facilitate smooth movement. If the chest wall is punctured and air at atmospheric pressure invades the body, the lung nearest the hole will collapse. If the pleural linings become inflamed, as they do in pleurisy, they lose their slippery nature and the lungs rub against the chest lining, making breathing painful and difficult. Normal lungs "breathe" with no perceptible friction.

How do the lungs fill up properly, normally, balloonlike, with air? Through muscular mechanisms.

The first is obvious. The muscles of the body's rib cage, known as the internal and external intercostals, act to expand the chest. These are the muscles used in thoracic breathing. The ultimate expression of thoracic breathing is a puffed-up chest.

The second way that muscular mechanism works to fill the lungs is less visible and very important. Between the bottom of the lungs and the top of the abdomen lies the diaphragm. This large, membranelike muscle is one of the hardest-working muscles in the body, and like the heart its toil is perpetual. Relaxed, the diaphragm is in the shape of a dome, arching up into the chest. When it contracts, it flattens out downwards, pushing the abdominal organs down and creating a vacuum in the chest cavity. Air rushes in and expands the lungs to fill the vacuum. When the diaphragm relaxes, it rises and creates excess pressure in the chest cavity, pushing air out of the lungs. When diaphragm and intercostal muscles work in harmony, as in abdominal breathing, efficient, even, full breathing results. If the diaphragm does not move slowly or contract fully, shallow, somewhat ragged thoracic breathing results.

The internal abdominal muscles also affect breathing. The psoas muscles tighten with emotional stress. As stress is released, the psoas muscles relax.

The amount of air delivered by diaphragm and chest varies widely during the day. Lying quietly in bed, you need to inhale about eight quarts of air per minute. Sitting up, about 16; walking, 24; running, 50. Not all of the air in the lungs reaches the bloodstream, however. Up to a third of the lungs consists of "dead space," pockets in which fresh air is not exchanged. The deeper and more fully the lungs are filled, the greater becomes the ratio of useful air-exchange space to dead space—another good reason for abdominal breathing.

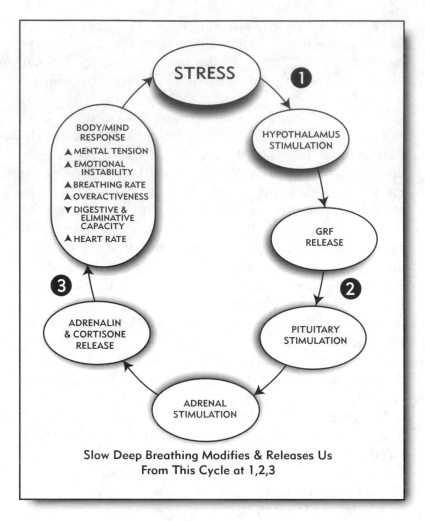

STRESS

❶

HYPOTHALAMUS
STIMULATION

BODY/MIND
RESPONSE
▲ MENTAL TENSION
▲ EMOTIONAL
    INSTABILITY
▲ BREATHING RATE
▲ OVERACTIVENESS
▼ DIGESTIVE &
    ELIMINATIVE
    CAPACITY
▲ HEART RATE

GRF
RELEASE

❸

❷

ADRENALIN
& CORTISONE
RELEASE

PITUITARY
STIMULATION

ADRENAL
STIMULATION

**Slow Deep Breathing Modifies & Releases Us
From This Cycle at 1,2,3**

The bronchi branch out from the trachea, the tube con-
necting the throat to the lungs, and divide, like the feeding
roots of a tree, into nearly countless tiny bronchioles. At
the end of the bronchioles is the locus of vital gas exchange: millions of tiny air sacs called alveoli. These micro-
balloons are surrounded by a fine network of blood vessels
called capillaries. When red blood cells reach the capillaries, they release carbon dioxide into the alveoli and absorb

oxygen. The carrier of gases in the red blood cells is the hemoglobin molecule. When blood circulates from the lungs back to the tissues of the body, the hemoglobin releases oxygen to the cells and picks up the waste carbon dioxide. The cells need oxygen to create energy efficiently and to carry out their functions. *This is why we need to breathe.*

The alveoli are thus of critical importance in keeping you alive. The processes of breathing and blood circulation meet at the alveoli, which must have sufficient surface area to provide the necessary oxygen. For the average healthy individual this should not be a problem. Nature provides each of us with about 300 million alveoli. Spread out flat, they would cover an area of more than seventy square meters—the floor area of a small apartment.

Trouble starts when smoking is taken up or heavy air pollution is encountered. Tobacco and marijuana smoke and other pollution account for almost all of the serious respiratory diseases. These irritants, mixing with the air breathed, invade lung tissue and damage the alveoli. The membranes lining the alveoli are thin and delicate, as they must be to exchange oxygen and carbon dioxide with the blood. They are easily victimized by smoke, which breaks them down and causes the normally tiny chambers to combine and form larger ones. A loss of total surface area results, and there is decreased efficiency in oxygen exchange. Smoke also causes alveoli to collapse. The lungs lose not only surface area and efficiency but elasticity as well. When large areas of lung break down in this manner, the insidious disease that has been parasitically building up for years makes itself known as emphysema, a crippling, life-threatening condition. Expelling air now takes a prodigious effort. Physical exertion is out of the question.

Elasticity of the lungs is essential to the up-down motion of abdominal breathing. If you have never smoked, or if you quit and let your lungs repair themselves over time, you will have enough elasticity to allow your diaphragm, in its natural movement, up-down, up-down, to massage your internal organs. Most people find their breathing capacity and elasticity begin to return to normal within six months; most lung tissue repairs itself within one to two years.

When the diaphragm contracts downward, the peritoneal sac containing the abdominal organs is compressed. Contraction compresses the blood vessels in those organs; the blood that is squeezed out returns to your heart that much faster. When the liver is thus massaged, bile moves out quicker, helping in detoxification. During exhalation, abdominal organs move up, expanding. Oxygenated blood from the arteries rushes in efficiently, and the abdominal cavity is cleansed and flushed. This boost to the circulatory system also increases the efficiency of the heart; it works better when more blood returns to it.

The heart also benefits physically from the general massaging action of abdominal breathing. The pericardial sac that surrounds the heart is attached to the diaphragm. As the diaphragm moves up and down, so does the sac, massaging the heart.

FIGHT OR FLIGHT

The "fight-or-flight" response is basically the primal, physiologic urge to defend or to flee in times of danger. Dr. Hans Selye found that even minor stress can be devastating to internal organs, especially to the adrenal glands and to the cardiovascular system. Because most stress is psychological, fighting or fleeing is usually of little value. We build up tension fueled by the release of adrenaline and cortisone from the adrenal gland. Eventually, the internal physiology of this reaction becomes pathological and we become more susceptible to heart disease, ulcers, stroke, irritable bowel, kidney disease, headaches, back pain, anxiety, and fear, plus diseases of deranged immunity such as cancer and forms of arthritis. Any weak system or organ in our body can eventually be ravaged by overresponse to stress, leading to serious disease or early death. We can stop the cycle through breathing: through the release of endorphins; through the release of melatonin from the pineal gland; and through mechanical effects of slow, deep breathing.

At the opposite end of the breathing spectrum, far from the peaceful abdominal massage, are the ragged gasps of fear.

When one is in a situation that is challenging or frightening, perceptions stimulate the hypothalamus, part of the ancient limbic system at the core of the brain that helps to regulate emotion and motivation. The hypothalamus emits a hormone that stimulates the pituitary gland to release substances that in turn excite the adrenal gland to release adrenaline (epinephrine) and cortisone. Adrenaline, in turn, stimulates the heart to beat faster and the vessels carrying blood to the muscles to open. The vessels that run to the digestive and eliminative organs constrict.

Blood pressure goes up.

More blood is being pumped, but many of the vessels have constricted, slowing the flow of blood.

Pupils open wider.

We breathe faster, shallower; or we even *hold* our breath.

The blood is shunted systematically from the vegetative organs to the muscles, preparing us to fight or take flight.

If one remains in this psychologically stressed state hour after hour, day in and day out, heart rate continues in an accelerated mode, the smaller blood vessels go into spasm, and breathing becomes erratic. As blood is shunted away from the digestive and eliminative systems, the kidneys perceive that the blood pressure is indeed lessening. (Throughout the rest of the limbic system, however, blood pressure is rising.) The kidneys may react to lower blood pressure by releasing a substance called renin. Renin, in turn, stimulates the release of the hormone angiotensin, which contracts the blood vessels, further raising blood pressure. When one is stuck in a chronic stress cycle, blood vessels are in chronic spasm and the delicate capillary network can rupture. A greater risk of arteriosclerosis, hypertension, heart disease, and stroke develops.

There is a breathing tactic that is useful in lowering blood pressure. We call it the Pressure-Reducing Breath. It utilizes one of the body's pressure-regulation mechanisms, the carotid bodies. These bodies are located along the carotid arteries in the neck, the arteries that supply blood to the brain, which is a glutton for oxygen—it consumes 20 percent of your supply when you are resting.

THE PRESSURE-REDUCING BREATH

1. Sit in a comfortable position in a quiet place.
2. Relax with a few Abdominal Breaths—four in, eight out.
3. Inhale about two-thirds lung capacity for a count of four.
4. Hold for a count of eight.
5. Exhale for a count of eight.
6. Continue Steps 3 through 5 for five to ten minutes. (Inhaling only two-thirds lung capacity will keep this breath from unintentionally raising your blood pressure during the holding phase.)

Practicing this technique daily, twice a day if possible, will aid significantly any plan to keep blood pressure in line.

When you hold your breath for a short time, the carotid bodies "think" blood pressure is going up, because breath-holding creates tension. They emit an alarm that causes blood vessels to dilate and leads to a drop in overall pressure. When breath-holding is incorporated into the basic Abdominal Breath, blood pressure falls because of the relaxing effect, and stays lower. (*Warning:* People with a history of stroke, heart disease, or very high blood pressure *must* consult their physician before using breath-holding techniques, which initially can cause a rise in blood pressure.) The Pressure-Reducing Breath, when used in conjunction with diet and exercise, is especially good for those people who have mild hypertension. (Avoid if you are prone to low blood pressure.)

ENDORPHINS

In addition to slowing your pulse and lowering your blood pressure—both very healthy goals—breathing techniques can initiate chemical antidotes to the stresses of tension and distress. This is accomplished through the release of chemicals with an opiate-like effect called endorphins. They are produced and released naturally in the brain. Studies have shown that during the process of slow, deep breathing the released endorphins cause a feeling of general well-being and relaxation.

Endorphins apply a brake to the hypothalamic fight-or-flight response in a situation of imminent danger. They keep things from getting wildly out of hand. A hunted animal, for example, experiences a surge of adrenaline, yet, because of an endorphin flood, chooses the proper direction of flight.

Endorphins not only temper response to dangerous situations, they also direct one through such situations without momentary distractions of pain. Rock climbers may remain undistracted by, or even ignorant of, cuts on their hands until the climb is over. A skier friend of ours reports that he badly scraped an arm when he took a nasty fall while slaloming through a forest one morning; he didn't notice the extensive abrasion until he had returned home that evening. In times of war or other disasters, people may become inured to pain because of endorphins.

You need not go to extremes to release endorphins. You don't have to enter the lion's cage to go one-on-one with basketball's Shaquille O'Neal. Endorphin release, as we say, can be stimulated by practicing slow, deep breathing techniques. When you are studying for an exam, physical danger is not a threat—but anxiety over eventual performance may be. Through channeled breathing, the student can release endorphins, be more relaxed, and study more effectively without the distractions of anxiety. Peak performance is within reach once again.

Laughter may release endorphins. Endorphin release may be part of that good feeling one has after a hearty laugh. The mental calm and relaxation that endorphins nurture certainly allow the body to heal more efficiently.

THE NOSE

Another important aspect of the physiology of breathing is the effect of breathing through the nose alone. It is much more beneficial to breathe through the nose than through the mouth. Thousands of hairs inside the nose, both visible hairs and the microscopic hairs called cilia, filter the air breathed through the nose. (The waving action of cilia rejects trapped mucus filled with dirt.) Blowing one's nose is the final step in the protective process. The nose knows: it constitutes the front-line defense against air pollution.

When air enters the body through the nostrils, the nasal turbinae (bones of the nasal passage), and the throat, it is warmed and humidified. By the time it reaches the lungs, it is at about body temperature. Lungs are more efficient with warm air. This fact can be demonstrated easily. Go outdoors on a cold day. Through your mouth, gulp frigid air into your lungs. You will feel a tightening, a core tension from antagonized lungs. When engaging in strenuous physical activity in cold weather, you must adjust to the temperature.

Breathing through the nose directly affects the central nervous system. Nerve receptors in the nose are part of the olfactory system; in other words, they are our sense of smell. But the olfactory system does more than transmit odors to the conscious mind. It is linked with the evolutionary, ancient limbic system that controls emotions and motiva-tion. The limbic system was seen in action when the fight-or-flight response was examined—a predator's scent in the air triggered immediate reactions in the nervous system of potential prey. It is the part of the brain most dominant in less evolved forms of life, the forms that operate purely on instinct. There is some scientific evidence to suggest that by manipulating nasal breathing, it is also possible to build energy, induce relaxation, heighten awareness, even en-hance creativity. Breathing unequally or alternately through the nostrils does the trick.

It sounds amazing, but it shouldn't. It is simply another case of taking advantage of natural breathing patterns, of placing them under conscious control.

As it is, there is a tendency for one nostril to predomi-nate over the other during the course of the day. Most healthy people will unconsciously switch the dominant nostril from time to time. This cycle has been confirmed by scientifically controlled studies. You can demonstrate it to yourself. At various times during the day, gently stop up one nostril with a thumb, then the other nostril. You will easily discern through which nostril the air is flowing more smoothly.

How does all this relate to the central nervous system? Research on brain function and structure during the past two decades has revealed that the sides (or hemispheres) of the brain have separate general functions. The right side of the brain, which controls the left side of the body, is the center of creative, nonlinear processes, such as intuition, design, art, music, and imagination. It is also the center of integration and receptivity. The left side predominantly controls rational linear processes, such as thinking, speak-ing, and writing. From it flow detail and order and focused activity. One hemisphere is not superior to the other, and the integration of both is needed for reaching full potential.

At different times, however, one hemisphere or the other may dominate our functioning. It is advantageous to control this dominance in order to meet the needs of a particular activity. Controlled breathing may prove to be the key to such control.

Research accomplished at the University of California at San Diego indicates that the nasal breathing cycle corresponds to the dominance of the left or the right hemisphere of the brain. The researcher David Shannahoff-Khalsa suggests that the cycle of hemispheric dominance could be manipulated by using breathing techniques: "Closing the right nostril and forcibly breathing through the left nostril produces greater EEG [electroencephalograph] activity in the right brain, and vice versa. These changes in the pattern of EEG dominance occur almost instantaneously; at most, they require periods of about five minutes. Occasionally, after ten or fifteen minutes of this breathing exercise, a permanent shift occurs."

What this means is that there is now a tool with which our state of mind can be adapted to the task at hand. A few minutes of breathing through the right nostril better prepares a person for mathematical or language-oriented work. A few minutes of breathing through the left nostril summons creative powers. "There is a true science of breathing," Mr. Shannahoff-Khalsa notes. "Discovering this is like finding a new sense."

With the use of the electroencephalograph and other sophisticated instruments, medical science seems to be converging with some ancient traditions of breath control. Long ago, yogis discovered that the right nostril (left brain) is the fiery or heating nostril and the left nostril (right brain) the cooling nostril. Breathing through the right nostril creates more heat in your system; breathing through your left nostril helps to cool you. Try it.

Using specific-nostril-breathing techniques can be difficult if the nose is stuffy or runny. There are simple techniques, aside from blowing one's nose, that can be employed
to open the nostrils without resorting to medications, which
work only for some people anyway. The mechanisms by
which these methods function are still unclear, but there is
no reason they should not be tried.

If your left nostril is stuffed, feel the lower part of your
skull, or directly beneath it, where the bone ends about half
an inch left of center. You will find a spot there that hurts a
little bit if you press on it. Rub your thumb gently around
this spot for ten to fifteen seconds. You should begin to feel
your sinuses clear.

Another way to effect this clearing is to put pressure under
the armpit on the side opposite to the nostril that is blocked.
Apply pressure for ten to fifteen seconds. For maximum effectiveness, press your armpit over the back of a chair or the
support span of a crutch. You may be surprised by the results.

The discovery of the connection between the nasal cycle and
the cycle of hemispheric dominance in the brain helps to explain
the effectiveness of the ancient yogic practice of Alternate Nostril
Breathing, which instills balance and clarity, and integrates mental faculties. Instead of boosting one cerebral hemisphere or the
other, the Alternate Nostril Breath stimulates both hemispheres
equally, suspending momentarily the cycle of hemispheric dominance. As with some other breathing techniques, this one should
be practiced when you are sitting comfortably and won't be
disturbed.

THE ALTERNATE NOSTRIL BREATH

1. Do a few relaxing Abdominal Breaths in a sitting
   position and stretch a bit to get in the mood.
2. Close your right nostril with your right thumb and
   inhale through your left nostril for two counts.
3. Close your left nostril with your right fourth finger and

hold your breath for a count of eight. (Both nostrils
are now closed.)
4. Open your right nostril and exhale through it for a
   count of four.
5. Inhale through your open right nostril for a count of two.
6. Close your right nostril and hold your breath for a count
   of eight.
7. Open your left nostril and exhale through it for a count
   of four.
8. Repeat Steps 2 through 7 for five to fifteen minutes. Use
   a timer to mark the minutes; otherwise, you will keep
   peeking to see how time has passed. Make your counts
   slow and consistent. If you feel fidgety, rock slowly
   back and forth. (As with any technique that involves
   breath-holding, you must consult with your physician
   on Alternate Nostril Breathing if you have a history of
   heart disease, stroke, or high blood pressure.)

Alternate Nostril Breathing becomes easier over time.
Ultimately, the calmness and clarity gained will continue
through the day. You may even experience lights, colors,
and sounds. Don't be alarmed; they are merely representa-
tions of the movement of energy in your body, and are as
natural a phenomenon as dreaming.

The Alternate Nostril Breath appears simple, but some
people find it difficult to sustain. The overactive mind may
rebel against the calming procedure. Stick with it even if
you feel distracted or fatigued; the rewards can be ample,
such as in dealing with coughs, asthma, poor concentration,
and memory loss.

CEREBRAL MASSAGE

Certain vigorous breath techniques like Kapalabhati and
Ha! have an interesting physiological side effect: they
"shake" the brain.

This is not as startling as it sounds. The brain floats in a
well of liquid called cerebrospinal fluid. The pressure of this

fluid goes up and down with the breath and chest cavity pressure. During inhalation, there is an increase in pressure within the chest. This tends to impede venous blood in its return from the cranium, raising slightly the pressure of the cerebrospinal fluid. During exhalation, pressure within the chest drops. There is a greater return flow of venous blood from the cranium, decreasing the pressure in the cerebrospinal fluid. The Kapalabhati Breath, with its rapid exhalations and abdominal pumping action, causes rapid changes in chest-cavity pressure. There is fluctuation in the cerebrospinal pressure—a kind of brain massage. The benefits of this phenomenon have yet to be proven scientifically, but there seems to be a cleansing effect on the central nervous system. (The word Kapalabhati means "skull cleanser.")

PURIFICATION

Whatever the final connection may be, it is in one's interest to practice optimal breathing for another simple physiological reason: as organs of elimination, lungs help to rid the body efficiently of toxins. *Through optimal breathing the overload of toxins can be prevented in the first place.* This advantageous effect operates even at the cellular level. Anatomically, the respiratory system is composed of the organs engaged in breathing: the nose, the mouth, the windpipe, all parts of the lungs. On a cellular level, respiration is the reaction that takes place in each of the 60 trillion cells in the body when carbon dioxide and oxygen are exchanged. When breathing is optimal, sufficient oxygen reaches all the cells and a state of aerobic metabolism develops. But through aging and diseases like emphysema and the loss of elasticity of the diaphragm and chest, chronic breathlessness occurs. When cells suffer a lack of oxygen, there is a buildup of carbon dioxide. Cells may have to fall back upon anaerobic metabolism to complete their tasks. Energy production without oxygen is inefficient—it is only one-sixteenth as efficient as aerobic metabolism.

Anaerobic metabolism makes possible strenuous efforts such as fast running. It should not be relied on for mild activities like typing, cooking, or ambling down the block to the corner grocery. Not only is anaerobic metabolism less efficient, it entails a buildup of lactic acid in the tissues. Toxic waste problems, as well as respiratory distress, develop. Inefficient breathing, along with smoking, pollution, lack of exercise, and chronic stress, decreases vitality on a cellular level.

The good news is that the process can be reversed; aging can be slowed, vitality restored. All you have to do is avoid as much smoke and pollution as possible, take regular exercise, and practice breathing techniques aimed at enhancing flexibility of the diaphragm and chest. Relief is only a breath away.

CHAPTER THREE

BREAKING THE CYCLE OF STRESS

Life is in the breath. He who half breathes, half lives.
—Ancient proverb

T he modern life is the tense life.

We are all too familiar with high-level stress points: divorce; serious illness; death of a loved one; relocation to a new job and to a new home, to a new neighborhood halfway across the country; theft of the family automobile; pressing deadlines on the year's big project on which everything rides. They stand out in high relief.

We are subjected as well to a barrage of low-level stresses. They are omnipresent and chronic, infiltrating our lives day and night: visual and invisible and now verbal pollution; boredom; constant interruptions; the office gossip with the nosey ears; the whir of an air conditioner hour after hour all night long; the cigar smoker in the elevator. The list, alas, is endless.

The more urban the society, the greater the probability of multiple combinations of stress. The social institution of the traffic jam is a perfect example. We sit there enveloped in poisonous air, our ears and brains and nerves assaulted by a cacophony of impatient taxicabs and grumbling trucks. We meet with frustration at every turn and cross-street. If we are especially unlucky, the jam escalates to its ultimate expression: gridlock. In some of our most crowded metropolises, even "peoplelock" has become a source of anxiety. The area around Bloomingdale's department store on New York City's hustling East Side is said to be the densest stretch of sidewalk in the Nation. Shopping there, one must endure the baleful provocations, real or imagined, of a crush of strangers.

Reaction to stress can compound irritations. Tempers are lost. Things are fumbled. Horrendous mistakes are made. One feels inundated. Decreased performance brings on more worry, more agitation. Tension feeds on itself. Life becomes more unpleasant, briefer.

The National Heart, Lung, and Blood Institute reports that a person's reaction to stress is every bit as significant a factor in the risk of heart disease as are hypertension, high blood cholesterol, and cigarette smoking, all of which are aggravated by tension. Stress can cause a rise in blood pressure. It can drive a person to strike a match to yet another cigarette. It can motivate a raid on the refrigerator for a fattening snack. These reactions to stress continue a cycle, with inner and outer stress factors reinforcing each other.

The stress cycle is reflected in breath. When you are enduring stress, you tend to breathe shallowly. The carbon dioxide level in the blood rises and the oxygen level goes down. You begin to feel a need to breathe harder, so you can rid your body of built-up carbon dioxide. But stress puts a clamp on your breathing apparatus. As the diaphragm tenses, abdominal and intercostal muscles constrict and you lose the ability to inhale deeply and naturally at the very moment you need it most. The respiratory system is locked in a state of tension.

Not all stressful events can be banished. But the stress-tension cycle can be broken. Reactions to stress can be transformed from tension, anxiety, and fatigue to a healthy, focused vitality that allows you to understand and overcome the problems that seep into your life. Yes, it all can be done through breath.

Breath, in fact, appears to be the most convenient way to combat emotional reaction to stress. Even the medical community is beginning to recognize breath control as an effective agent in stress management. The *Journal of the American Medical Association (JAMA)* reported the use of slow, deep breathing as an element in effective stress-management programs for patients with ischemic heart disease—that is, with blocked blood flow. For these patients, stress management is literally a matter of life and breath. For the rest of us, it is a matter of prevention.

How is it that something as simple as breath control helps a person feel better and live a healthier life?

Breath control is *convenient*. Direct, voluntary control can be established quickly. Direct control over functions such as heart rate, blood pressure, and body temperature is not achieved easily by the conscious mind. Physiological functions have been manipulated by means of biofeedback and yoga, but years of discipline are required to become adept at yoga, and biofeedback requires bulky, expensive machinery. Breath is controllable; in turn, it improves, albeit indirectly, functions of other physiological processes. Most important, practicing specific techniques periodically will lead to a shift in breathing pattern, even when you are not aware of it.

The effect of slow, deep breathing on the other automatic functions of the body temper and reverse the stress-induced fight-or-flight response. This familiar phenomenon is deeply rooted in physiology. Ages ago, when our forebears roamed the plains and forests of Africa, this biological alarm mechanism meant the difference between life and death, between hunger and a fresh kill to roast at the campfire. (Mel Brooks avers that the main source of propulsion in those days was fear.) Nowadays, few of us are hunting or being hunted in the forest, but we react to stressful situations in the same way our ancestors did. This ingrained reaction does not, however, prepare us for the typical modern challenge—the job interview, the overnight term paper, the unexpected dinner for six, the desperation of finding a parking space as curtain time nears. To meet such challenges we must be calm, focused, confident—and ready. Patience is a virtue, particularly in the brutal face of frustration. But it is next to impossible to be patient when the response includes the rapid, shallow, thoracic breathing process triggered by the biological alarm response. By the power of association, the habit of thoracic breathing keeps baseline tension high.

In fact, tension can be summoned easily, even in a calm situation, by calling up rapid, shallow breathing. Try it. Make yourself breathe short and jerkily for a couple of minutes. Do you feel like taking on the world? It's quite the opposite of calm and collected breathing, isn't it!

Remember the newborn baby? It doesn't have a care in the world. Its breathing is deep and slow and rhythmic. Its abdomen is relaxed. Its lungs fill easily and fully. Nature intended us to breathe like that all the time. If reactions to the constant stresses of life weren't overloading our circuits, the process would be sustained the way it was when we took our first breaths. But life requires reactions. The overly tense thoracic breathing habit develops early in many of us and is reinforced constantly. As soon as a child realizes that there are expectations of him, first from his mother, then from others, he learns to become what he is not in order to get what he needs. Because he is acting in ways contrary to

his nature, tension is generated. Breathing becomes shallow, restrictive, and held.

The traumatic quest for mother's love is only the first situation in a life choking with stressful situations. According
to Dr. Harold Jackson of the Greenville Hospital System in
South Carolina, possibly half of the nation's children are
plagued with psychosomatic illness related to stress. Day-
time-wetting, headaches, and stomachaches are common
symptoms of childhood stress. Stress begins early in life.
Possibly half of the presenting complaints in a physician's
office have a psychosomatic component, either primary or
secondary. Colic, for instance, may be a symptom of stress.
Early experiences pile up as life rolls on. Overall tension
increases as the ways in which it is expressed change with
growth into adulthood. Even harmless little episodes, daily
occurrences, may hold the potential for trouble.

The feeling is a familiar one. Something trivial has got-
ten you all worked up. You can't remember whether the
Statue of Liberty holds the torch in her left hand or in her
right hand, or if the cover of the book she is cradling reads
"July 4, 1776" or "In God We Trust." Or it's lunch hour and
you're waiting in line in a busy "fast" food restaurant for the
special of the day. The line snails along. The cashier
appears to be even slower than normal—it's her revenge for
having to take the job—and is needlessly incompetent.
Other customers are grousing. You shift your weight
uneasily. You tap a foot. Impatience causes your breathing
pattern to quicken. All you can think of is how much of
your time is being wasted. With every fiber of your being
you want the line to HURRY UP, GET A MOVE ON UP
THERE!! But all *that* does is speed up your pulse. Your
blood pressure rises, your head throbs. Short, jerky breathing compounds your frustration and anger. Because it takes
time to calm down, what's left of the lunch hour is shot.
Such reactions to waiting—no matter where—cost a great

deal in terms of lifespan and health, not to mention the day-to-day quality of life. Learning to breathe appropriately in response to a trying situation can be of extraordinary value. Coping methods like the basic Abdominal Breath provide an alternative to the biological alarm reaction.

All of us wait in line in many places—at the bank, the post office, the Xerox machine, the supermarket, on the road, and so on. So much of our so-called free time is spent waiting, impatiently, angrily. There is a simple tactic to take advantage of—and to make the best of—the inevitable. It is called the Waiting Peacefully Breath. It allows you to release the tension of waiting and to experience peace and non-rushing in the experience. By being able to relax in a waiting situation, you gain patience and the fulfillment that comes from enjoying having nothing to do but to be kind to others around you and to yourself.

THE WAITING (IN LINE) PEACEFULLY BREATH

1. Do the slow, deep Abdominal Breath with long, relaxed exhalation. Feel impatience drifting away. (In a traffic jam, don't breathe too deeply.)
2. Continue the Abdominal Breath. As you relax, realize that impatience will not get you to the head of the line any faster. Impatience only makes the time seem longer. (A watched pot never boils.)
3. See those around you as fellow human beings also waiting and working to the best of their ability.
4. Hum or sigh to yourself for a while.
5. Imagine how pleasurable it would be if everyone around you were also relaxed and trying new ways to be patient and efficient.

Using the Waiting Breath, you can begin to reverse the biological alarm response with as few as three or four conscious breaths. By the time you reach your destination, you might even be smiling.

Yes, *smiling*, as we and our clients have experienced.

By initiating a calming response whenever you are confronted with a stress-provoking situation, you can turn the problems of daily life to your advantage. Calming yourself, as a matter of fact, can be habit-forming. Traffic jams, bus rides, and long lines become opportunities to develop and reinforce beneficial breathing.

The lengthy exhalation is the keystone of the Waiting Breath tactic. This is how it works:

When you are in a calm, resting state, functions such as pulse rate and blood pressure rise and fall in a cyclical pattern that corresponds to respiration. When you inhale, the activation cycle picks up; resting muscle tension increases slightly and pulse rate and blood pressure rise. As you exhale, these indicators ebb.

Do a few slow, deep breaths with lengthy exhalations, feeling your pulse at the same time. Automatic functions like heart rate and blood pressure are influenced naturally. Many breathing techniques center on slowing exhalation.

Another aspect of breathing directed for health and pleasure is continuity. The process should be rhythmic and smooth. In other words, an even breath, no breaks, no interruptions in the flow. Medical research has shown that a ragged breathing pattern is associated with risk of heart disease. Patients in Minneapolis who had suffered heart attacks had breathed in a shallow, uneven pattern, relying chiefly on thoracic breathing.

In fact, a state of tension, with no strenuous physical outlet available, affects more than breath and heart; the entire organism strains to no avail. Muscle tension, joints, digestion, and elimination suffer. When the arousal trigger is chronically pulled, one's insides grind away. An individual at constant odds with himself is like the driver of an automobile with one foot on the accelerator and one foot on the brake.

When you initiate breathing for relaxation, you will notice that not only do you reverse the fight-or-flight response, you may avoid it all together.

Say you are driving to a crucial job interview early in the morning after a troubling night's sleep and nothing, absolutely nothing, is going right. You hit every red light. You are cut off by rude drivers. The drawbridge is stuck in the up position. You *could* get angry and focus on those frustrating realities, fueling anticipation of your imminent lateness. You could become frantic, taking risks and putting yourself (and other drivers) in jeopardy. Instead, you take a wise course. You focus on your breathing. Arriving at your destination late is inevitable, but it shouldn't make a big difference in terms of landing the job. (The interviewer may be tardy, too.) However, your appearance and mood, when you do arrive, will make a difference, maybe *the* difference. A relaxed, coherent applicant will be much more impressive than a breathless, sweaty one who has just had a frantic race with the clock.

Breath can be employed against the common tendency to take stress home in the briefcase.

One often arrives back at his doorstep too keyed up to enjoy the rest of the waking hours. If it's been rough out there on the road or at the office or at the factory or at the counter, you might (without really wanting to) pick a fight with your spouse, yell at the kids, boot the dog, or drink too much. Or all four. For some people, anger and temper tantrums lead to physical abuse. In any case, they can ruin the quality of life in an instant and leave everyone feeling upset and uninspired.

Breath awareness is of vital importance in heading off such trouble. When you find yourself becoming irrational or getting out of hand, shift to slow, deep breathing. You will be able to express yourself in a more civilized way—and everyone will breathe easier for it.

To shed that bored, lifeless, frustrating feeling that the work routine can bring about, why not try a regular after-work strategy? With just a little more time than you need for the simple Abdominal Breath technique, you can take advantage of the Stress-Discharging Breath.

THE STRESS-DISCHARGING BREATH

1. Make sure you will not be disturbed.
2. Get into a comfortable position, lying down or sitting in a favorite chair. Loosen any constricting clothing.
3. Start relaxing with several Abdominal Breaths; breathe in to the count of four, breathe out to the count of eight.
4. Take a deep breath through your nose and hold it. Tense your feet as long as you can. (*Warning:* If you have a history of heart disease, high blood pressure, or stroke, consult your physician about this tech nique. He may suggest a modified version, with little or no breath-holding.)
5. Relax your feet as you exhale with a sigh through your mouth.
6. Take a few deep Abdominal Breaths to the count, as in Step 3.
7. Breathe in deeply through your nose. Hold it. Tense your calves.
8. Relax your calves as you breathe out with a strong exhalation.
9. Repeat the sequence for each area of the body, working from the extremities to the center: feet, calves, thighs, buttocks, abdomen. Next, the upper body: fingers, forearms, upper arms, shoulders. (Hunch your shoulders up to your ears.) Don't forget your face; it may hold much tension. Work it in three stages: pull your jaw back so your mouth looks funny; scrunch up your nose; furrow your brow.
10. Take a few minutes to relax and let go.
(Prolonged breath-holding can cause a transient rise in

blood pressure. This is why we include a cautionary note with the Stress-Discharging Breath, and with some others. Even if you do not have any of the health conditions referred to, you still may want to modify the exercise to include only a brief hold of the breath. This brief hold presses slightly on the carotid bodies in the neck, causing blood pressure to go *down*.)

For discharging stress during the workday, when there may not be much time or appropriate space, there is a technique that is quick and convenient: the Cleansing Breath. It releases carbon dioxide from the lungs. This in turn helps to lower the body's acidity, automatically creating relaxation. Experiments have demonstrated that the more acid in one's body chemistry, the more tense one tends to become.

The Cleansing Breath can be used routinely during the day. It is a secret weapon that will help you meet any challenge. Imagine this scene. An important meeting in the board room looms. You sit at your desk and try to collect and organize your thoughts. What else can you do to ready yourself?

THE CLEANSING BREATH

1. Inhale deeply through your nose.
2. Exhale through your puckered mouth, as if you were blowing out a candle.
3. Repeat Steps 1 and 2 three times.
4. Issue a few sighs. Inhale deeply, then sigh. Again. Again. With each sigh, drop your chin to your chest and droop your shoulders. Think of yourself as a tire letting all its air out. Think of the tension you are releasing.

With a relaxed body and a clear mind you are ready for the business at hand.

Using tactics like the Cleansing Breath, you can release tension at intervals through the day. If you think of accumulating tension as water filling a bucket under a leaky faucet, it is obvious that you will have an easier time handling matters if the bucket is emptied periodically. This surely is better than letting the bucket fill to the brim or to overflowing, then having to lift the heavy load to the sink. Letting your "bucket" fill up weighs you down with an unmanageable load of tension at the end of the day. Why not empty the bucket every hour on the hour!

But sometimes stress comes on so strongly that one feels attacked on all sides. Even the elevator slides right by your floor. This is the time to initiate the Shielding Breath, a technique to help you release the feeling of impingement.

THE SHIELDING BREATH

1. Do thirty to sixty seconds of the Abdominal Breath.
2. Imagine yourself enveloped in a protective white light as you begin to relax.
3. Inhale the light to bolster the experience.
4. Exhale fears and anxieties. Feel the light washing them away.
5. Surround your space in this white light.

In only a few minutes, you will find that you have shifted from an island of fear and anxiety to the turf of calm strength. You will probably discover that most of the stress was inflated well beyond reality—mountains out of molehills. With the Shielding Breath, the stress regains its proper proportions.

Breathing techniques can be used over a period of days to prepare for a tension-provoking event, like a final examination in school.

Examinations are usually times of high tension. Many students tend to react to the prospect with a fight-or-flight response. What is needed for success is quite the opposite—

calmness and control. By channeling breath, a handle on the situation can be acquired.

Successful use of breathing in this example starts well before the test. The basic Abdominal Breath prepares the student for calm, effective study of the material he needs to know. It confers the added advantage of associating the subject matter with a state of relaxation. (Soothing music, such as the favorite Pachelbel Canon in D, encourages slow, deep breathing and relaxation, which helps in the retention of information.) When the material has been studied to satisfaction, the student triggers in an imagery tactic. The Abdominal Breath with the count—four in, eight out—can be used to enter a state of calm and clarity; the student imagines himself going through the exam confidently—knowing the information well and recalling it easily. An optimal frame of mind is being established. (Of course, this approach works only after the material has been reviewed thoroughly!)

While actually taking the examination, the student may still perceive it to be a flustering, high-pressure situation. If he starts to feel panicky, if he gets upset over a question whose answer he can't figure out, he should initiate a slow, deep, relaxing breath. He should focus for a half minute on calming himself down and clearing his mind while maintaining the rhythm of breathing. He will get a better perspective on the situation and be able to continue comfortably with the test. (Dr. Migdow used this technique to help get through medical school.)

The many uses of breath control are already an open secret. Most of us employ breath unconsciously to lift ourselves out of difficult situations. Remember sighing or taking deep breaths before tackling a big or unpleasant job? Or before asking your father if you could borrow the car?

An acquaintance of ours relates how he worked his way through college by washing dishes in the cafeteria on campus. The plates, cups, and silverware would come hurtling along a conveyor belt. The dishes would start backing up and hurling themselves suicidally off the counter and onto the floor. He found himself jumping about frantically, like Charlie Chaplin in *Modern Times*, desperately striving to save what he could. After each onslaught, there would be a slack period, and he found himself taking slow, deep breaths to calm down. Before long, when another army of kamikaze dishes would assault the work station, this fellow instinctively took a few deep breaths to help him stay in control. He learned to deal with his labors without getting anxious and adding to the melee.

A chapter on stress would not be complete without mention of pollution, that ubiquitous low-level irritant. Even though the respiratory system is inside the body, it is effectively outside, because it collides with the environment with every breath we take. Like skin, lungs are extraordinarily sensitive to pollutants. Although many laws regarding pollution are in place and cigarette smoking indoors is banned almost everywhere, additional laws and regulations are needed, so it is well to take measures to mitigate the personal effects of pollution.

Obviously, there are situations in which it is advisable not to breathe deeply. To breathe deeply in an urban street is to risk inhaling concentrated pollutants. In road traffic, near buses especially, it is advisable to breathe shallowly. The carbon monoxide of vehicle exhaust is absorbed in the bloodstream about thirty times faster than oxygen. It combines avidly with hemoglobin in red blood cells, making those cells incapable of transporting oxygen. Shallow, slow, even breathing through the filter of the nose can make the best of a lamentable situation. It is advisable to relax the abdomen and fill the lungs only one half to two thirds.

Some sources of pollution are not readily apparent. "Sick" buildings are a growing problem. Offices and schools still have asbestos in their structures. Asbestos is a silent killer that causes asbestosis and cancer. Radon gas-ventilation is a solution. If you breathe deeply and feel worse instead of energized and relaxed, it may be that you are inhaling an invisible or an unrecognized source of pollution, such as asbestos. You may cough repeatedly, even though you don't have flu or a cold and you do not smoke. Breath can be the key to detection of the health threat.

In a palpably cleaner environment, you can, after exposure to pollution, resume deep breathing to relieve the burden of the recent pollution. Deep breathing keeps lungs and bronchial tissues flexible. As long as the lungs remain flexible, they can regurgitate any deposited pollutants and any mucus in which aerial pollutants were trapped.

Certain environments are naturally cleaner and healthier. They contain more oxygen, less pollution, and more negative ions.

Negative ions were researched by the U.S. Air Force in the 1940s and 1950s. Pilots passed out at high altitudes. Air in the plane was tested, and found to be high in positive ions due to the metallic, closed environment of the aircraft. When negative-ion generators were placed in the planes, pilots stayed awake and alert.

The seashore is awash in healthy ions. Woods are also high in oxygen-negative ions, because trees generate negative ions. Trees and plants absorb carbon dioxide and other toxic chemicals that create unhealthy positive ions. The more polluted an area, such as a large city with chemical pollution, a lack of trees, and stagnant air, the more positive ions are generated. These electropositive ions create an experience of tension and heaviness, sometimes even depression. Certain winds, the so-called "ill winds," actually carry positive ions. They can lead to disease and death.

BREATHING OCEAN AIR AND NEGATIVE IONS

The waves, ocean swells, and offshore breezes make sea air highly beneficial to your health. The actions of the water create negative ions—beneficial electric charges. These charges, brought into the body with the breath, tend to re-energize the whole system. Sea air also contains minerals. They are absorbed into the lungs, freshening and cleansing the tissues. Sea air, wet and pure, helps to relieve inflammation caused by gritty metropolitan pollution.

Negative ions are abundant during and after a rainfall. This explains why one usually feels particularly robust at those times. The rainbow seen after a rainstorm is the visual component of the deep sense of relaxation and well-being we feel in large part because of negative ions. Waterfalls also generate rainbows (thus the Rainbow Bridge at Niagara Falls). Water smashing against rocks creates the mist that refracts sunlight into a rainbow. In addition, the breaking up of the droplets generates a high concentration of negative ions. This may be one reason Niagara Falls is so popular a honeymoon resort. The ions supply get-up-and-go.

River rapids create negative-ion concentrations through the action of water dashing against rocks and exploding with crashing waves, reversals, and souse holes. The "ion high" experienced by whitewater boaters explains in part the addictive quality of the sport. In a canoe, a kayak, or a raft, river-running is thrilling, challenging, and just plain fun. When you are able, spend some time at the seashore or by a river and breathe deeply to take in revitalizing negative ions.

If you can't get to the ocean, you can create an oceanic atmosphere in your home with plants and negative-ion generators. Plants pour oxygen and negative ions into the air, and remove toxic substances, such as benzene, formaldehyde, and ammonia. Plants have the ability to do this in a scientific way. Negative-ion generators are machines that pour more ions into the air than plants do. They are helpful in ridding the site of soot, dirt, mold, and bacteria. Negative ions cause those substances to bind and fall to the floor, where they can be vacuumed away. These generators are quiet and small, and can be used in any room in your home to create a healthy, invigorating atmosphere.

If you have high-level pollution, because you live in a city or just painted or laid new carpeting, you might want a negative-ion generator combined with an air purifier.

If you have a lot of mold in your home, you can get an ion generator that emits ozone, which kills the mold.

These generators are employed in some malls, with plants and waterfalls, creating a healthy atmosphere. In airplanes, the generators could pacify the toxic air.

May we suggest that you contact a health store for information on negative-ion generators and air purifiers.

Your respiratory system has millions of microscopic hairs called *cilia*. They constantly trap pollutants and irritants through inhalation. They "wave back" pollutants and secreted mucus until you are able to cough them out or blow them out your nose. One of the worst aspects of smoking is that these little hairs are killed, robbing the individual of a vital defense. Breathing techniques like the Lung Expander and the Lung Strengthener help to keep lungs flexible and capable of self-defense. The stress-induced habit of shallow thoracic breathing makes the muscles and tissues of the chest and the diaphragm "rust away" because of disuse; they then tighten up, inhibiting flexibility.

Ridding oneself of pollutants and tension is not always easy. When you first undertake breathing and stretching exercises, like the Stress-Discharging Breath, toxicity is liberated from joints, muscles, and interstitial tissues. It enters the bloodstream for release through the kidneys and skin or for metabolization in the liver. Freed of this pollution, you may feel tired and headachey. This is not an uncommon epilogue; it is a sign of recovery from a sludgy state, a blessing in disguise. In holistic medicine, this is known as a cleansing or detoxification reaction. The unpleasantness passes presently and you will feel much better.

To repeat: *The most important thing to keep in mind about breaking the stress cycle is that breath can be used for an enhanced integration of life's experiences. There is a connection between breath and daily activity. Integrate and simplify experience while using breath.*

Alyson Herbine, a stress-management counselor in Philadelphia, told us, "So much happens so quickly and simply for stress-management students when they practice breathing exercises. Most of them have forgotten the ability they had as children to 'let go.' The deep peace and stillness that pervade the room after they practice are followed by quiet, trusting self-disclosures. It is a dramatic contrast to the anger and defensiveness expressed at the beginning of class. No matter how often I have seen this, I always re-experience with them their amazement and relief—a joyous communion of new friends.

"From my own practice I know that the nervous system is strengthened and steadied by breathing techniques. The mind becomes clearer, emotions are defused, and detachment gradually develops. Regular practice brings predictable results."

CHAPTER FOUR

BREATHING BREAKS

I'm just breathing these days, building up oxygen so I can dive again into the deep waters.
—Carlo Rubbia, Nobel Prize-winner for work in atomic physics

Breathing breaks give me a terrific jolt, terrific energy. They are the most important thing in my life—they really are. They keep my life going. I had no idea to what heights I could keep bouncing.
—Interior designer, mother of two, grandmother of two

Breathing breaks are quick injections of fresh air into your day.

Breathing breaks slip easily into daily routines: walking, working, dishwashing, car-waxing, typing, eating—anything, anywhere.

Breathing breaks are a conscious extension of a natural tendency. By spending a bit of time each day staying in touch with the potential of breathing, you can make your life richer and more harmonious.

When you're at work, do you occasionally stand up, yawn, and stretch? (Did reading the word "yawn" just now make you yawn?) You *should* stand up and yawn and stretch from time to time if yours is a sedentary occupation. A yawn is a kind of automatic breathing technique. It usually is initiated by a buildup of carbon dioxide in the blood. When this waste gas reaches a certain level of concentration, the yawning reflex is triggered. (*Now* are you yawning? Yawning can be initiated by suggestion, sometimes by mere mention of the word. Now?) Yawning feels good because it stretches facial and neck muscles. When the shoulders are pulled back and the chest expands, the diaphragm stretches as well. As the yawn stretches the muscles related to breath, it releases stale air from deep down in the lungs.

Another breath technique that can be applied is humming. When one feels good, humming happens naturally. It releases air in a slow, continuous, steady way and leads to automatic relaxation. In addition to reflecting a happier mood, humming in itself is pleasurable. It can even make those around you feel upbeat.

People who have sedentary jobs benefit the most from breathing breaks. Trapped in an office, stuck behind the desk for hours, sitting in the same place at a machine, people get numb, their muscles tighten up, stale air accumulates. Many of the means commonly employed to counteract "deskitis" are not as effective as supervisors like to believe. Take the coffee break. For many people the coffee break tends to reinforce the stress response. Caffeine has a bipolar effect—first it lifts you way up, then it drops you way down. Sensitive people find themselves enervated but jittery. We urge you to abolish self-defeating cycles and substitute the clean energy of relaxed breathing.

Here's how a conscious breathing break works:

THE WORK-STATION BREATHING BREAK

1. You are at your work station. Put aside pencils, pens, calculators, and other tools. Turn off the word processor. Put your calls on hold.
2. Uncross your legs and relax in your chair. Sit up straight. (Most people tend to sit on their lower backs,

concentrating the full weight of the upper body on one
vertebra.)
3. Take slow, deep breaths.
4. Allow your abdomen to fill up completely with oxygen.
   Exhale.
5. Repeat Steps 3 and 4 for a minute or so.
6. Mentally scan your body. Scan slowly from your head
   to your toes, part by part, area by area. Head, shoulders,
   neck, back, arms, buttocks, thighs, calves, feet, toes.
   Note the spots that are tense. Focus your breath
   directly into those spots. You may want to move the
   affected areas if you can: shrug your shoulders, for
   instance, or move your neck, or wiggle your toes.
7. Feel aches and pains released as you exhale.
8. Experience the areas relaxing and opening as you inhale.
9. Return—relaxed and revitalized—to what you were doing.

Try the technique here and now. If time allows, repeat it
a few times.

Do the Work-Station Breathing Break—or any of the
other breathing techniques that are appropriate—every
hour on the hour. You will find that taking two minutes for
a breathing break—120 ticks of the clock—can relax, energize, and clear your mind, making the hour that follows productive and pleasant, releasing stress and tension that have
built up in the past hour. The psychology of the break is
that of the "zing"—the quick, clean fix that regenerates the
groggy mind or the tense body, a restoration to peak performance levels.

Here's how a computer analyst in Montreal employs
breathing breaks to overcome work-related difficulties:

"Working with a computer terminal and typing as I stared
into a video monitor led to pain. At the end of each day, I
began to find myself plagued with sore eyes and a stiff neck
and achy shoulders. I began to suffer chronic pain in my
back, right shoulder, and right arm. I found it almost impossible to continue normally with the job I am trained for and

like very much. Breathing breaks now get me through any indisposition. I relax by sitting in my chair and letting my shoulders and arms fall into a relaxed mode. I breathe in deeply through my nose, raising my head and shoulders while inhaling. While exhaling, I let my head and shoulders collapse. Repeating the exhalation-inhalation process relaxes me overall and eases any pain in my shoulders and arms. Six years of discomfort are a thing of the past. I'm like my old self again, eager to get to work each morning."

A lawyer has told us, "Because of the very demanding nature of my profession, I experienced considerable stress while at the office and was dead tired by the end of the day. By practicing deep abdominal breathing for ten minutes before going to work and for one to two minutes every hour while at the office, I am able to experience a calmness that is surprising. Such breathing significantly lowers the stress to such a level that I am no longer tired or drained of energy at the workday's close."

Breathing breaks hold great promise for the business world. If they could be established company-wide, payoffs could be enormous. Health, both on and off the job, is of continuing concern to cost-conscious companies. A huge paper manufacturer has spent millions of dollars on a fitness and health center for employees. Breathing breaks take only a few minutes' time and cost nothing. Not a thin dime. They are a perfect plus in a corporate fitness policy.

Ask yourself what all forms of healthy exercise have in common. Right you are: rich, deep, sustained breathing. Breathing breaks keep employees healthier and on the job, and boost individual morale. Practiced together several times a day, breathing breaks bring about a periodic release of group tension and create a common bond. This means less job-related stress, more enjoyment of work all around, and, perforce, increased efficiency.

Nobel Laureate Ilya Prigogine states in his theory of dissipative structures that when parts of a whole act together, a greater strength occurs and a shift in perception and values can occur for the whole group. It is true for systems from atoms to societies. If everyone in the workplace takes a break as a unit, the expanded efficiency and mutual respect can be remarkable.

Breathing breaks in the classroom serve both to enhance teacher-student relations and stimulate creativity while relieving anxiety and stress. Such breaks can be introduced into a child's first school experience. Going from home to nursery school is such a dramatic change from what had been the normal day near the maternal apron strings that breathing for stress reduction is a beneficial adjunct to the traditional breaks for milk and (sugarless, please) cookies.

As every teacher knows only too well, children become fidgety after sitting at a desk for a bit of time. Breathing breaks drain off restlessness. They're great fun when done in unison. The young scholars walk around, stretch, wiggle their shoulders. Some teachers make a contest of wiggling. Wiggling and stretching help children become more comfortable in a group setting. The students now are better able to focus on their schoolwork.

"WIGGLE MONSTER" BREAK

1. The children wiggle their bodies, starting with fingers and feet, then going on to their arms and legs until they're wiggling all over.
2. They laugh and giggle, releasing any tension from their bodies. Laughter is a natural tension releaser.
3. The children slow their wiggling gradually, then do abdominal breathing for a few moments.
4. Teacher and students talk about how much fun they have had, how well they feel, how much better things are.

As the boys and girls progress through the grades, breathing breaks can be linked with lessons in language and speech, in the connections between breath and the production of sound. The internal mechanisms of stress and their damaging effects on the body should be understood. Breathing breaks are an excellent way of introducing this vital knowledge; they lay the groundwork for developing the ability to work with one's emotions.

Breathing breaks are also perfect for use in the home. The person who cannot devote time and concentration to sustained exercises will be well served by concentrated and focused breaks. They can upgrade all aspects of life: in the morning at home, throughout the day at school or work, at night before going to bed.

THE RELAX-AND-LET-GO BREATH

1. Get in a comfortable sitting position.
2. Do a few head-rolls slowly and gently in a counter-clockwise direction as you breathe deeply.
3. Do a few more head-rolls, clockwise, slowly and gently. Play at letting go. Avoid forcing.
4. Inhale and pull your shoulders up.
5. Hold your breath, hunching your shoulders.
6. Exhale and drop your shoulders.
7. Repeat Steps 4, 5, and 6 four or five times.
8. Roll your shoulders forward while inhaling and exhaling.
9. Roll your shoulders back. Continue inhaling and exhaling gracefully, not quickly, not slowly.
10. Take a deep breath and exhale, making a Ha! sound.
11. Repeat Step 10 three or four times to release deep tension and re-energize yourself. (Prior to sleeping, skip Steps 9 and 10.)

With the Relax-and-Let-Go Breath, you are letting it all go in order to relax. Whenever you feel like leaving your tensions behind, plunge into this breath.

Never forget that breath is the interconnection in every-thing you do.

"An annual physical checkup when I was feeling over-worked, tired, and burned out" led Jean Saunders, a psy-chotherapist with a busy private practice in Rocky Hill, Connecticut, to our suggestion that she try Abdominal Breath breaks after a session with a client. "It is six months later now," she's written to us, "and while I still experience tiredness and stress—my work is demanding—I find that the breathing break is immediately rejuvenating: it relieves tension and makes me more alert in meeting the next client. And it's such a simple technique."

CHAPTER FIVE

PEAK PERFORMANCE

*In a tight situation remember that deep breathing
clears the mind and relaxes the muscles.*
—Jeff Lowe, The Ice Experience

Peak performance!
This is performance at its best, when it is better than you thought it ever could be—*and* you've enjoyed every minute of it. Peak performance is energy in harmony with activity. When that harmony is missing, peak performance is impossible.

All of us have had days when everything hummed along beautifully, when everything went right, nothing went wrong, only to be followed by disastrous days when everything we touched fell apart. In our research into performance states, we wanted to discover the emotional and the psychological factors causing such fluctuations. We wanted to learn, for instance, why a basketball player could be like Grant Hill one day and all but inept the next. Or why a business executive could be impressive at Tuesday's sales meeting and a dud at Wednesday's.

Initial research examined fifty peak athletic performances. Male and female athletes were invited to describe, in as much detail as they could, their finest moments on the playing field. They were asked to visualize those moments as vividly as possible, to re-create the emotions and the feelings of the experience, and to write them all down. We wanted to know what it was like from the *inside*.

The athletes were also asked to compare their peak performance with their worst effort. What was the quality of their emotional climate when they were playing poorly?

An analysis of the reports was a paradigm of the Ideal Performance State. Organized into categories, it adds up to the explosive energy and drive of a peak performance, no matter what the activity. The primary categories were as follows:

THE ABILITY TO FEEL RELAXED AND LOOSE-MUSCLED. A tight individual consumes a tremendous amount of energy and is an inefficient performer. One can be tight and tense and not even be aware of it. Extraordinary individuals tune in to their muscles and achieve a state of low resting tension. While walking or working or playing—or anything—only those muscles necessary for getting the job done should be employed. The other muscles should be left in a state of relative relaxation—ignored.

A FEELING OF INTERNAL CALM AND QUIET. In our fast-paced, agitated society, it is easy to believe that a speedy and accelerated mental state must accompany top performance. In fact, the opposite is true. Research repeatedly reveals that mental calm and quiet are associated with best performance, physical or mental. A calm mind correlates with a low-range alpha brain-wave frequency. It has been shown that slow deep breathing with focus on the breath can shift the person from hectic beta waves to calm, focused alpha waves. The higher the frequency of one's brain waves, the more quickly one starts to feel frantic.

Order unravels. When breathing is slowed, a calming psychological state is in control and one starts to concentrate well and feel confident.

LOWERED ANXIETY—A PRESSURE-FREE CLIMATE. It is difficult, if not impossible, to perform optimally when one is feeling anxious. But the feeling of anxiety can be controlled. Anxiety, after all, is a perceptual problem. Through regulation of breath, the mind can be reached and altered. One can switch easily out of the ragged, shallow breathing pattern associated with anxiety and into a deep, steady, confident breathing pattern that provides an efficient oxygen supply, thereby shucking any gripping elements.

A FEELING OF HIGH ENERGY. This presents an apparent paradox: relaxation, inner calm, virtually no pressure—yet a simultaneous feeling of high energy. It is a specific kind of energy, both pleasant and powerful, fueled almost exclusively from positive emotions. It is the kind of feeling one has when one is enthusiastic, inspired. In its purest form this energy can be referred to as joy. One wants to go with the flow. In its intensity this energy can become euphoric. Proper breathing is essential for this state, because full oxygenization is vital to feeling and sustaining high energy. Specific centers throughout the body supply the individual with continuous productive energy. As muscles contract with tension, they act like a steel net that interferes with normal circulation of energy. Negative or depressing thoughts and nervous actions also drain off enormous amounts of energy; they are as exhausting as a long day of hard labor. One must focus on efficient action and good feelings; they invigorate and "feed" the psyche.

OPTIMISM AND POSITIVISM. A person who is feeling pessimistic and negative can never produce a satisfying performance.

A FEELING OF FUN. Simply put, if a person can create a climate of enthusiasm and enjoyment, he is more apt to per-

WHICH CELL ARE YOU?

HIGH ENERGY

A	B
(*Smooth, deep, full breath*) High energy, positive feelings Alert, energetic, lively, stimulated, vigorous, enthused, high team spirit Relaxed muscles, calm mental state, focused, in control *Peak performance—best chance of good performance*	(*Tight, jagged breath, out of control*) High energy, negative feelings Nervous, fearful, anxious, angry, frustrated, upset, vengeful Tight muscles, accelerated mental state, tunnel vision *Second best chance of good performance*
C	**D**
(*Easy, relaxed breath*) Low energy, positive feelings Tired, fatigued, weary, exhausted, out of gas, low desire Relaxed muscles, calm mental state, unfocused (spacey) *Third best chance of good performance*	(*Shallow, erratic breath*) Low energy, negative feelings Bored, disinterested, annoyed, irritated, seriously lacking motivation Variable muscle tension, variable calmness, unfocused *Worst chance of good performance*

PLEASANT ← → UNPLEASANT

LOW ENERGY

form at his peak. Some people tend to get this notion backwards; they believe that if they perform well, they will have fun. *Enjoyment must precede achievement.* Peak performance comes after an internal climate of fun and pleasure has been established, not the other way around.

We are talking about a psychologically controlled state of mind. The Ideal Performance State does more than facilitate the activity; it helps to insulate the person against the potentially devastating stresses of life, both psychologically and physically. Energy is turned outward to meet the challenge, rather than inward. Enervating tension is channeled away.

On the preceding page is a model developed for visualizing energy states that helps to comprehend optimal performance.

Four equal-sized energy cells are arranged to form a square. Down the center of the square is a line; this vertical axis represents the fluctuations of energy from high (at the top) to low. The horizontal axis represents the range of emotional feelings, from pleasant (on the outer left edge) to unpleasant (on the outer right edge). The pleasant end corresponds to positive emotions, the unpleasant to negative emotions. Using this two-dimensional pattern, many things about performance as it relates to stress become clearer.

Cell A, the upper-left box, is the high-positive-energy cell. It coincides with the Ideal Performance State. The emotional climate in Cell A is pressure-free, but motivation is high. Resting muscle tone is relaxed but ready for action. Breathing is full, deep, smooth. There is the seemingly paradoxical combination of calm and intensity.

Cell B, the upper-right box, is the high-negative-energy cell. Here, too, there is intensity, but the experience is not pleasurable. High motivation is accompanied by nervousness, anxiety, or anger. The pressured emotional climate is often one of frustration, even vengefulness. Muscles become tight, tight, tight, even during rest breaks. Breathing is apt to be rapid and ragged, even out of control. Energy is usually misdirected. The best performance recorded in the high-negative-energy cell has reflected only 60 percent of perceived ability. There are disastrous performances in Cell B.

Cell C, the bottom-left box, is the low-positive-energy cell. The emotional climate here is pleasant, but motivation and commitment are lacking. Breath is easy and relaxed, but lack of energy leads to a variety of problems with concentration. This easygoing state all but guarantees a mediocre performance at best.

Cell D, the bottom-right box, reflects low negative energy. The emotional climate is one of boredom, apathy, annoyance. Muscle tone is erratic; breathing, for the most part, is shallow. Performance is abysmal.

According to the athletes themselves, every one of the two hundred peak performances were Cell A.

The next step was to learn how to focus quickly on performance states and move into Cell A if the performer is "boxed out" of that cell.

One psychologically illuminating approach to high energy states is to conceive of them in terms of the colors with which they can be associated. Some athletes in the research program found this to be an ideal approach. High positive energy (Cell A) seems to be associated with the color blue. As befits the ultimate state of peak performance, blue connotes calmness, relaxation, warmth, and depth. People who practically live in Cell A, seeing blue, are productive people. They live long lives. Even though the pace is frantic at times, they stay healthy. They like what they do. They are so devoted to what they do that stress responses are channeled into the drive to do better rather than into worry and complaints. Bob Hope is a perfect example of the Cell A personality. In the demanding, fast-paced world of show business, the comedian has been one of the most popular and one of the busiest. At this writing, he is a vibrant nonogenarian. He is the epitome of calmness and relaxation. His flawless timing flows from an inner harmony.

High negative energy (Cell B) seems to be associated with the color red. When one "sees red," he is receiving a critical alarm signal. The fight-or-flight response is running out of control. It is time to effect measures to restore equilibrium and to channel intensity.

The real test of a top-drawer performer is what he does in adversity. Does he panic? Does he set off his biological alarm response? Does he thrust himself into Cell B? Many people can be adequate performers in Cell B, but it costs dearly; full potential, as we have noted, can never be realized.

Dwellers in Cell B rarely enjoy what they do—life is a war for them; it is hellish for those in Cells C and D. Cell A performers are able to regulate themselves sensitively. They transform adversity into challenge, tackling it with enthusiasm and intensity. Although the world whirls chaotically around them, the As' energy experiences are satisfying. One physiological reason that people do not perform well with negative energy is they are so busy coping with fear, anger, and anxiety that they cannot discipline tension. It remains in their systems, sapping their spirits.

When we say "breath is energy," we are referring both to the aerobic drive and the psychological lift that proper breathing provides and to the ability to make available any energy formerly wasted on excess tension. Energy is not being created; it is being liberated. Only in a positive emotional state, only in Cell A, can potential be fully freed.

Breathing is a mirror of emotions. Conversely, conscious manipulation of breathing patterns can change emotional states. When one takes charge of his breathing patterns, dramatic changes occur. By equalizing breaths, especially by taking deep and prolonged breaths, an entirely different, healthier emotional climate can be realized.

It is important to remember that one has learned, con-sciously and unconsciously, to repress some emotions, putting them out of reach of influence. When these emo-tions resurface through conscious effort, they are likely to be the kind that accompany high *negative* energy or low *negative* energy. In addition, the large reservoir of emotional energy has been effectively blocked. Using breath to access and control emotions is not easy at first; one is not used to doing it. But over time a vast source of energy and vitality that formerly went to waste will be regained. When the nature of breathing in some of the most extreme emotional states is examined closely, insight is gained into the con-nection between emotion and breathing. On the verge of crying, a person experiences a fear of releasing unpleasant emotions. That fear breaks loose during the cry. It is jetti-soned all of a sudden—*whoosh*! There is a burst of tears and there are jerky motions in the chest and abdomen. Crying is a perfect application of a natural breathing technique. It stimulates lungs and abdominal organs. It provides a kind of overall massage. It washes the inner environment. It releases destructive emotions.

There's a breathing technique that releases a cleansing cry. It can be used when a secret grief is being held back, because there is a terror of experiencing it. It also revitalizes and refocuses energy. This ancient technique is called, in Sanskrit, Kapalabhati. It literally cleans and purifies the sinus and nasal passages and the respiratory tree. It is also known to stimulate digestion and elimination, activate the solar plexus, and stimulate the nervous system. This tech-nique is a non-caffeine, non-sugar method to increase vitality in a calm way. The calmness comes in part from the fact that the fast action of Kapalabhati causes vibrations in the cerebrospinal fluid, thus giving the brain a gentle massage. Give it a try right now if you feel like having an experience of relaxed vitality. The successive past-forceful exhalations while squeezing the abdomen is the action that produces the staccato, pumping sensation.

KAPALABHATI: THE ENERGIZING BREATH

1. Sit in a comfortable position.
2. Do one or two minutes of the Abdominal Breath and the Relaxation Breath.
3. Inhale fully.
4. Expel short, forceful exhalations through the left nostril while pulling in your abdomen with each exhalation. You will experience a staccato exhalation until your lungs are fully emptied.
5. Repeat full inhalations and staccato exhalations ten times; any inhalation between staccato exhalations should be involuntary and passive.
6. Inhale fully.
7. Exhale fully.
8. Inhale about three-quarters lung capacity and hold it as long as comfortable, then exhale. (If you have a history of heart disease, high blood pressure, or stroke, release the breath slowly instead of holding it. A person with epilepsy should never deep-breathe rapidly.)
9. Repeat Steps 4–8 through the right nostril.
10. Finish by repeating Steps 4–8 simultaneously through both nostrils.

Some people who really get into Kapalabhati have sensations of tears and emotions pouring out. They feel much freer, much calmer, like the clear, cool calm after a summer thunderstorm. No longer at odds with themselves, they are again free to function optimally and with full clarity of mind.

Laughter is another natural breathing technique, and it has a cleansing and revitalizing effect similar to Kapalabhati's. It originates in the solar plexus, the abdominal area that was considered by the sages to be the "seat" of bodily energy. The magazine editor Norman Cousins wrote that he literally laughed his way back to health after being at death's door. He watched hours and hours of comedy films. In Japanese terminology, Cousins merely stimulated his *hara* center over and over again, raising his healing energy and effecting a "miraculous" recovery. (The *hara* center is two inches below the navel; it is where the upper and lower halves of the body are joined.) Patch Adams, M.D., the physician on whom the recent Robin Williams motion picture was based, relates countless stories on the way he uses humor to help people with illnesses overcome depression and disease. He has worked with thousands of patients and given numerous seminars to health professionals on the healing power of humor and laughter. Laughter shifts the frame of mind from anxiety and negativity to self-confidence and joy. Health practitioners have found the positive attitude of joy and self-assuredness to be an important element in true healing. Laughter is no laughing matter.

It is intriguing to note that although our culture has a propensity for chest breathing, recognition of the beneficial nature of abdominal breathing is inescapable. It is deep in the vernacular. A real joke gets a "belly laugh." "Letting it all hang out" makes one feel good all over. One might even laugh so hard that he cries—another significant release of tension. Breathing techniques simply make use of tendencies and processes that are already present, transforming them to advantage.

Mood can be modified through breath. The next time you feel tense and uptight, do the basic Abdominal Breath. Tensions should fly away. If you feel sad, try the Ha! Breath that follows; it is designed to revitalize you. It is an aid in experiencing and letting go any down feelings. Ha! does not block the emotional state. Rather, it raises energy, helping you become mentally clear while experiencing the emotion. In a state of clarity it is easier to trace the internal and the external causes of the sadness, to discover ways to work with the causes in a life-affirming way.

Ha! Breathing also is applicable to a broad variety of situations, such as in the martial arts and weightlifting. It works by stimulating the hara center. The hara center is felt to be the energy center of the body in Oriental philosophy and practice. Its center is located approximately two inches below the navel. It is accessed consciously in the arts of akido, kung fu, and karate, and in many forms of dance and music. Great singers sing from their hara, or gut. The hara center is easy to access through this technique. By stimulating this center, we gain a tremendous increase in the amount of energy in the body, raising our day-to-day performance and speeding healing processes. This is one of the few breaths in which you purposely exhale through the mouth. Mouth exhalation strengthens the force of the breath.

THE HA! BREATH

1. Tilt your head up and inhale deeply through your nose.
2. Exhale forcefully through your mouth—issue a loud Ha!
   sound that originates in your lower abdomen as you
   thrust your head and body forward at the waist; your
   hands slide down to your knees. (You will want to
   make a quieter or even a silent Ha! sound in situations
   where barking is not appropriate.)
3. Repeat the Ha! Breath as needed. (*Warning:* If you have
   a history of heart disease, high blood pressure, or
   stroke, go easy with this breath; transient rises in blood
   pressure can occur during Ha!)

You may want to do ten or even twenty repetitions on a daily basis. Some days, you may want to do the Ha! Breath only as needed. An excellent time for a Ha! is before meals; it tones the digestive organs.

Just as the Ha! Breath energizes, the Relaxation Breath can calm an overwrought state and transform anger into creative energy. But remember, the road to optimal performance isn't always easy.

When a breathing technique is used to convert emotional energy, particularly while working intensively with significant problems and blockages, hidden and unrecognized emotions can unexpectedly surface. If a problem has been denied or pushed out of consciousness, breathing techniques can bring it to the fore at a time when leisure, privacy, and inclination permit dealing with it. Some people, taught to suppress their feelings, understandably have difficulty with such exposure and purification. But research has shown time and again that it is unhealthy to let basic feelings, whether they be of anger or hatred or even love, go unrecognized.

Fear often leads to a socially ingrained perfectionist attitude. Breathing techniques can come to the rescue here, too. One perfectionist, a woman, had trouble even trying out the breathing techniques we suggested. She felt inhibited and told us, "These are silly," and began to laugh. Without realizing it, she was close to doing the Ha! Breath. When this was pointed out to her, realization of the pun (Ha! and laughter) made her laugh harder. Her stomach moved up and in with each expulsion of breath. The lightbulb in her head clicked on. She had suddenly comprehended what we were saying. She is today a faithful, enthusiastic practitioner of breathing exercises.

Often (as in the story above) there is a natural route around inhibitions from which the value of breathing techniques can be demonstrated. In addition to laughing and crying, singing and yawning are natural body activities through which the body deepens and normalizes breathing. When you sing, you focus your breath, you concentrate on sound, you align your entire breath apparatus. When you sing with gusto, you employ tremendous inhalation and exhalation as well as vigorous, loosening movements of diaphragm and chest muscles. You feel better after singing. You have expressed yourself. You have relaxed through deep, regular breathing. It is as simple and profound as that. Put a song in your heart right now. Sing in the shower, in the car, or on a walk.

Singing even provides a lift in situations of great pressure that one might think not appropriate for bursting into song.

Ice climbing is a chilling sport. The consequences of a mind going out of control can be serious. The ability to relax in tough circumstances confers an essential advantage. It is for this reason that Norman Kingsley, an experienced mountaineer and the author of *Icecraft*, a technique manual for climbers, recommended that "when you get that strange feeling that this is all wrong, that you are committing voluntary suicide, start trying to sing the words of a song that you have trouble remembering the lyrics for." Trying to recall the words takes the climber's mind off fear. The singing or humming to fill in words not remembered bends breath to the rhythmic sonority of the song, slows it, makes it regular. The ragged gasps of fear drop away, action becomes deliberate, calm, effective.

Breath is internal music. It is our ebb and flow. Through experiencing this harmony, all processes are facilitated.

Many people do not realize that through stretching and breathing in a certain way, "known" limits can be exceeded. One can go through life unnecessarily getting progressively tighter and stiffer with age. Just as a certain tension level is set in muscles, a tension level is set in mind—levels that inform us as to what limits cannot be exceeded.

Limits are not set in concrete! Barriers are false, illusory. Deeper relaxation, serenity, peace, and vigor can be reached through training in breathing. Psychological limits *can* be stretched. A prime example was the "unreachable" four-minute mile. Once Roger Bannister did it, everyone, it seemed, was able to do it. Today, we don't give a sub-four-minute mile a second thought.

As we stated at the start, a brief period of time is enough to confirm all this. Breathing is a tool that enables anyone to perform better in every aspect of life. We can't emphasize that enough. Through controlled, directed breathing, you can be more open and loving with your family, learn more in your schooling, be more effective in business, jump higher, run faster. New-found vitality lifts creativity. A whole new realm of experience, power, self-control, and performance is yours, as you simultaneously gain in calmness, awareness, compassion, and forgiveness. Yes, you, too, can perform optimally.

We admit that the implications are remarkable. Mastery, from a series of techniques that cost nothing to learn, nothing to use, are an integral part of your life. They are totally in your control. They can be done anywhere, anytime. As a friend exuberantly told us while reading a draft of this manuscript, "Breathing is the most important thing in my life—now I know why."

CHAPTER SIX

THE SPORTING LIFE

The sedentary modern life has left a gap in our essence, a physical interval that can be filled with the joy of sport. One can jog to revitalize heart and lungs, or go sea-kayaking to restore a lost sense of wonder and breathtaking adventure, or play one-on-one basketball to score "feel better" points. Sporting activities can breathe new life into life.

"But," you counter, "I'm too busy. The pressure at the shop leaves me frazzled. Late meetings interfere. When I get home, I am inundated with moral obligations, family and all that."

Arnold Schwarzenegger is said to experience a suffocating schedule constriction. When he ended his former professional career—body-building—and entered the business world, the daily healthful workouts he was accustomed to had to be benched in favor of cross-country trips, paperwork, and seemingly endless meetings. But he was determined to stay in shape and in tip-top health. How did he do it? He made time. When business has him on the run, he calls a time-out and, we are told, gets in an aerobic workout. We can all be just as inventive.

If you don't care for jogging or your doctor prohibits it, there are dozens of other activities you can indulge in. How about rollerskating? Kinesiology researchers at UCLA discovered that rollerskating for five hours a week confers significant health benefits. Seventeen men and women who took up the sport enjoyed an increase of 18 percent in maximal oxygen consumption. Leg strength improved 23 percent. Cholesterol and blood pressure readings were reduced.

Brisk walking is another excellent exercise for keeping your body moving well, your bones and muscles in youthful condition, and a spring in your step.

We have detailed the Ideal Performance State in relation to breathing. Let us now review the role of breath awareness and the coordination of breath with particular sports. There are ways that you can improve your level of play and enhance your enjoyment of your favorite sports.

Basically, breathing can help your endeavors in two ways. First, by practicing techniques already suggested, you will increase the vital capacity of your lungs; that translates into more fuel for the furnace. Second, you can channel breathing techniques into specific situations.

In actual play, if all is going well—if you are not serving aces or completing your passes—you should not be thinking about your breath. Most likely, your lungs are functioning naturally and efficiently. Your breathing techniques are there, waiting, like an invisible catapult, to be sprung at your adversary. But if things are not going well, you can go straight to your breath for answers and solutions—either to calm down or to improve a lackluster performance.

Let's say you become angry with an umpire or an opponent, or even at your own play. You plunge into a state of negative energy. You are distracted by your anger, and your game begins to lose its sheen. The more emotionally out of sync you become, the more your shots will land beyond the baseline. Your breath becomes harsh and ragged as you re-call yesterday's returns that were placed consistently deep to the corner of your foe's backhand court. There is a way to overcome your upset and regain your winning ways.

Instead of dwelling on your inaccuracies, take three deep breaths like the Relaxation Breath recommended for stress-ful situations. You will move quickly from a state of high negative energy to one of high positive energy. Amazingly, this rebound can be achieved instantly, between add-out and deuce or between an unforced error and the next serve. Focusing on breath, you will no longer be distracted by petty mis-hits. You go on to the next point centered in the present and playing for the moment.

The Centering Breath also works in any moment in which energy needs to be stable and calm.

THE CENTERING BREATH

1. Perform the Relaxation Breath, allowing your body to relax.
2. Imagine your inner self as a clear light.
3. Imagine your breath pulling you into this inner self.
4. Feel the calm and peace in this part of yourself.
5. Inhale stability, as if you are a tree growing roots.
6. Exhale fear and anxiety.
7. Look around to see how much more pleasant the environment is.

The Centering Breath takes about ten to fifteen seconds to do. Try it before the next point in tennis, before that big free throw with the basketball championship on the line, before your final dive from the high board.

Breath can be used to move quickly from a state of low energy to one of high energy. Let's say you are dragging yourself around the court, feeling hopeless and helpless. Instead of bellowing at the official or throwing your racket at the net or sawdust at a spectator, think about raising your vitality and intensity. Breathe. Perfect would be the Ha! Breathe, silently or out loud. The Ha! can be used even during play. (Better the silent Ha! then.) On the changeover, do a few Relaxation Breaths to calm the mind, then several Ha! Breaths to charge yourself back up. You will find yourself again playing vigorously. In fact, on a deeper level the purpose of Ha! Breathing goes beyond vitality to courage.

You may find yourself matched against an opponent who is better than you are, technically more accomplished, but there is no reason why you cannot boost your level of play. The Ha! Breath can help you summon courage to hang in there: as a quarterback facing a fearsome blitz; a mountain climber facing a sheer, icy pitch; a hockey goalie facing a one-on-one penalty shot; a baseball batter facing a fireballing southpaw; a golfer needing an eagle on a par-three hole to cop a sudden-victory playoff. The Ha! Breath summons up the guts and the intensity needed to transcend previous limits.

There's another technique that potentiates the effect of the Ha! Breath. Again imagine you are on the tennis court, this time facing a titanic opponent, and it's your service. Call on the Three-Part Breath, which is also called the Clavicular Breath, because it raises shoulders and collarbone (clavicles). It pulls in maximum oxygenation to the upper lungs.

THE THREE-PART BREATH
(CLAVICULAR BREATH)

1. Inhale and feel your abdomen expanding.
2. Keep breathing in. Feel your chest expand when the lower lung is filled.
3. Breathe into the clavicle area after the chest is filled. Feel your shoulders rising. (You've filled your lungs to the utmost, from abdomen to chest to shoulders.)
4. Exhale and drop your shoulders, relaxing them com-

pletely. (*Warning:* Do this technique only a few times; otherwise, you might hyperventilate.)

The Three-Part Breath leads to increased energy overall and reduces tension in your shoulders; shoulder tension interferes with the fluidity of arm motion, as in a tennis serve. (Now, as you serve, focus your intensity with a Ha! Breath. An ace!)

The Three-Part Breath is particularly effective when the chest is flexible and relaxed. One way to create more openness in the upper chest is to do the Lung Expander. A difficulty that our lungs have in doing their job optimally is that they are prevented from expanding to their full capacity by tension in the chest. This constriction, usually symbolic of protecting heart and feelings, not only decreases the amount of oxygen that can be inhaled, it squanders vitality through defensiveness and blocks a rich source of emotional energy. Just as Ha! Breath can unlock our physical energies, the Lung Expander can unlock emotional energies so they may be used for creativity and fulfillment in day-to-day lives.

THE LUNG EXPANDER

1. Spend a few minutes doing the Relaxation Breath to open the lungs.
2. Place your fingertips on the top part of your shoulders.
3. Inhale through your nose as you tilt your head back and bring your elbows up, out, and back, fully expanding your chest. (Don't force this stretching motion. You may feel some tension, but there should be no pain. Stretching should never be done to the point of pain.)
4. Exhale through your mouth, bring your head down, move your elbows forward, down, and in.
5. Repeat this sequence five to ten times, feeling the opening and vitality in the chest. Start slowly, then build up speed as the movement becomes coordinated. Remember to keep fingertips on your shoulders at all times.

If you do the Lung Expander daily, you will see a significant improvement in oxygenation in your sporting life.

OXYGEN DEBT

When should you start integrating breath technique?

In sports, the first step in breathing awareness is recognition of oxygen needs—needs that are constantly changing. To maintain efficient activity in aerobic sports such as running and tennis, oxygen consumed by muscles must be replaced constantly. During strenuous exercise, overall blood flow may increase up to sixfold, and blood flow to the muscles may increase thirty times. In the muscles, blood vessel volume may increase to almost one hundred times resting capacity in order to accommodate increased activity. In short, the body becomes a glutton for oxygen. If muscles consume more oxygen than lungs and the circulatory system deliver, an "oxygen debt" is incurred. Muscles must now perform some of their work using inefficient anaerobic metabolism. Lactic acid builds up. Muscles ache. There is fatigue, even anxiety—breathless anxiety.

Clearly, oxygen debt is not a condition anyone should experience for an extended length of time. If training strategy is proper, if it includes techniques like the Three-Part Breath and the Lung Expander, it can be all but avoided.

As a person becomes accustomed to gradually longer periods of exercise, muscles of the chest and diaphragm become more efficient and increasingly elastic. Breathing becomes easier, more fluid; less oxygen is needed for the breathing process itself.

In terms of volume per minute, aerobic training can triple breathing power. The heart works more efficiently. With each heartbeat, more blood is pumped, which is why highly trained athletes can be extremely healthy with a resting pulse of only 45 to 50 beats per minute. Most people clock in between 66 and 84.

Ask yourself what the oxygen needs are in the games you play. Is aerobic training right for you? Again, let's use tennis as the example. You can easily go from point to point without calling on reserves of energy and oxygen, unless a prolonged rally has you dashing around the court. When you have the chance to rush to the net and put away the point, will the energy and power be there? Through aerobic training, the advantage will be yours.

Incurring a minor but still annoying oxygen debt is in some cases a normal by-product of the warm-up. A friend of ours is accustomed to running without undue strain three or four miles several days a week. Before he sets out, he does a series of light, easy stretches and walks around for a while. This helps him get his system moving in stages from rest to high-end demands. (Walking calls on one and a half times more oxygen than is needed for just sitting; running requires more than three times the sitting amount.) When our friend begins his run, he feels fine. He hasn't consumed the oxygen still present in his blood after the warm-up. Gradually, though, that oxygen is used up and he needs all the oxygen his circulatory system can deliver. He comes to a hill. His heart and lungs are not yet operating at their fullest capacity. An oxygen debt accumulates. As he mounts the crest of the hill, he begins to feel fatigued. He experiences a few aches and pains. He starts down the other side. Because less oxygen is needed to run downhill, the oxygen debt is repaid rapidly. He is now fully warmed up. His heart and lungs are functioning at 80 to 85 percent of capacity. Beta-endorphins, secreted by the pituitary gland, are coursing through his bloodstream. He's beginning to feel that enviable sensation known as "runner's high." Our friend is enveloped in another pleasant workout.

Similar patterns of oxygen debt and repayment occur in other continuously aerobic sports like swimming and bicycling. Nobody can become successful in distance sports without developing the full, deep breathing attributable to the abdominal component of deep breathing.

In sports like tennis, football, and basketball, in which there are breaks in the action, time-outs can be used to re-pay an oxygen debt incurred by a fast break or a breathless rally or by the two-minute drill or bruising play under the boards. The Three-Part Breath is good for quick restoration of oxygen if action can resume at any moment.

FINE-TUNING THE BREATHING PROCESS

Fine-tuning the breathing process to fit the actual physi-cal course of movement can be done in two stages.

The first stage is to become aware of the breathing pattern. It may be necessary to have someone act as a mon-itor, observing and reporting; sophisticated counseling has become an intrinsic part of professional athletics. Of course, you might have enough physical self-awareness to monitor yourself. Ask yourself, Does my breathing pattern fit the rhythm of the activity?

If it's a game with many players, you will see for yourself that many of them breathe raggedly, in a fashion in no way coordinated with the flow of the game. Fast action is often accompanied by rapid, shallow breathing. We have seen some athletes hold their breaths while competing, incredible as that may seem. Breath-holding incurs a ruinous oxygen debt. Some breath-holders are unaware of their action and must be told they are doing it. Correction leads to better play.

In the second stage, breathing patterns must be adapted in ways relative to critical moments in the activity. These moments are often at points of contact or critical balance, moments when you *want* to breathe out smoothly. The exhalation accomplishes two things: it helps to reinforce the sense of rhythm and play, and it produces a state of low muscle tension at contact point. This lowered baseline tension provides a sense of harmony to muscular action and allows it more fluidity. Tension will decrease in muscles not needed for performance, while those consciously used when the ball is hit or the skis are turned or the trigger is squeezed will have more power available. There is no rigidity opposing smooth action. A relaxed general muscle tone makes more energy available. Tension is not sapping vitality. You are relaxing your muscles but not your mind. In fact, mental awareness will be heightened by this process, because you are experiencing less distraction.

ENERGY SINK

Rock climbing illustrates both the tension-created energy sink and how breathing can help us emerge from it. Imagine yourself, a first-time climber, at the practice crag. Though protected by the top rope (the securing rope from above), a beginner may be nervous and cling anxiously to the rock face. He may have only a rough idea of what moves to make. He grips the handholds harder than necessary, dissipating energy. His breath is ragged. His mouth is dry. He is experiencing what climbers call "sewing machine" legs; that is, his muscles, especially those in his legs, are vibrating, causing his whole body to shake out of control. Understandably, he is having second or even third thoughts about the enterprise and may ask to be lowered from the cliff after he has made only scant progress.

The experienced climber, on the other hand, moves boldly and rhythmically, in perfect balance with the elements. He moves at an easy pace—not too fast, not too slow. He employs just enough muscular force to keep himself in balance. If he is forced into an awkward position, he will hang with his arms extended so that his weight is taken on the ligaments and bones and not on the muscles, which could become painfully flexed. Whenever possible, he climbs with his legs, using his hands only for balance, conserving arm strength for use when necessary. By sparing energy and remaining calm, first-rate climbers can for a long time literally "hang in there" on what looks to be a near-impossible perch while plotting the next moves. Then, like a cat that has been waiting patiently for a mouse, the committed climber moves decisively, exhaling at moments of greatest exertion. If the pitch is at the limit of his ability, he may heave, grunt, gasp, even curse. When the most difficult step is past, he resumes regular, deep breathing.

Extreme situations reveal important aspects of breath control. Rapid gasps waste energy. The relaxation component of proper breathing saves energy.

SMOOTHING THE WAY

Returning to the less gripping world of tennis: it is best to inhale when you see the ball coming back at you and to exhale smoothly as you hit your return. Some players utter a silent word as they exhale—a word like "yes" or "smooth" or "free" or "easy." The word helps to calm exhalation.

After practicing the exhalation utterance out loud for a bit, you may merely want to form it mentally as you exhale. Some athletes grunt rather than speak—it's their way of exhaling consciously. Courageous Monica Seles issues a loud grunt to keep herself pumped up with breath. It works for her. Not everyone is a Monica, of course. We have learned that loud grunting contributes to muscle tension and distraction in some players. But a long, extended out-breath, sounding like ahhhhhh, produces the best results for most of us. Ahhhhhh.

In some instances we have recommended singing or humming during exhalation. It does more than substitute for a word or a grunt. Singing or humming supports relaxation through correct use of the respiratory system. It is perfect for people who are overly self-critical or obsessively

analytical. Such men and women have a great deal of difficulty "turning on the automatic," the feeling central to
excellence in athletics. In the ancient yogic system, repeating sounds or humming is called mantra. Mantras are used
to relax or invigorate; different sounds create different reactions in the psyche and body. "Om," for example, is relaxing. "Hai" is invigorating.

We have been told by athletes that when everything was
"going right" and their engines were purring, they had tunes
going through their heads. Chris Evert says a tune created a
natural rhythm for her. A skier colleague of ours tells us
that when "the music is good," the turns in the deep pow-
der of Utah are ecstatic. Internal rhythms prime the whole
human organism and keep it harmonized.

With people who have difficulty kicking over the automatic, we urge musical activity to induce the neurological
shift from a predominantly left-brain, logical, sequential
approach to a free-flowing, spontaneous, instinctive
approach characteristic of the right brain. No athlete can
reach full potential without activating the right side of his
brain. This has been shown in both objective and subjec-
tive studies.

We encourage some of our athlete-clients to hum at
contact points. Some tennis players have a hitch or a
pause in their service motion. If they hum audibly as they
serve, the hitch vanishes like a puff of smoke. Continuous
sound induces continuous motion. Whether it is a silent
exhalation, a word, a whisper, or a hum, it pays to exhale
at the critical points in the action.

Besides using breath to conserve energy, breath techniques can be applied as well to reducing or eliminating
that old bugaboo, pre-play tension. In this way, much
energy is conserved; how much is all but incalculable.
Some professionals are so anxious before a contest that
they vomit. Even the best preparation is diminished

when tension dulls the athlete's edge, especially the psychological edge. Simple relaxation breathing can relieve both individual athletes and teams plagued with major-league butterflies.

CREATIVE VISUALIZATIONS

The use of breath and imagery techniques can unlock your optimal life—and sports—potential. Further, they can help in any number of other ways.

Use of imagery with breathing for healing is a fascinating subject. The same sort of imagery can be used to relax your body. Imagine calm, cool energy flowing through each area of your body. Visualizing the color blue is helpful if such imagery is done in concert with relaxation breathing. This connects with color research on the Ideal Performance State.

Imagery with breathing helps to prepare one mentally for sporting activities. Consider how much time athletes spend getting ready physically for their event—practicing their sprints, running gaits, sparring, volleying—yet few of them ever think to prepare themselves mentally as well. Image-making with breathing is a simple technique that forges a link between mental and physical exertions. It works, regardless of the activity.

The Australian psychologist Alan Richardson confirmed that physical skills can be improved through "mental practice." Working with basketball players, he found that after twenty days a group that practiced free throws only mentally—they "pictured" themselves taking aim and tossing up the basketball—improved its scoring rate 23 percent, while a group that actively practiced for the same amount of time on the foul line—actually throwing the ball toward the hoop—improved by only one percentage point. A group that didn't practice either mentally or physically showed no improvement. At Cornell University, Richardson's study was refined. A group of dart-throwers imagined they were pitching darts. A second group only imagined watching themselves throwing. Both groups improved their scoring, but the former group improved twice as much. A group that did not practice mentally or physically showed no improvement.

You can combine imagery and breathing techniques yourself. Find a comfortable position, lying down or sitting. Do some relaxation breathing to induce the calm needed to engage in effective image-making. Focus on your body, on both its strengths and its weaknesses, and on the movements associated with the activity you are about to be involved in. Then plunge into...

THE FOCUSING BREATH

1. Do the Abdominal Breath two or three times.
2. Imagine yourself inhaling focus and vitality.
3. Imagine exhaling fogginess and tiredness.
4. Feel that you are alone with your task and that all else is superfluous—noise, movement, crowds, thought.
5. Take a deep breath in and out with an audible sigh.
6. Repeat the breath and let your shoulders drop.
7. Imagine performing the activity as smoothly and as perfectly as possible. Concentrate completely.
8. If you are preparing for a race, imagine yourself pulling ahead of the pack at a particular point and crossing the finish line ahead of all other runners. If you are about to go golfing, put yourself into the proper frame of mind by imaging yourself hitting the ball perfectly every time. The great Tiger Woods has used visualization techniques since he was a child. The image-making technique is a microcosm, a mental stimulation, of the event to be experienced.

Breathing applied in conjunction with imaging, or visualization, is a way to achieve by oneself the equivalent of posthypnotic suggestion. It can be applied at any time, and without the aid of an expert. The benefits are increased concentration, stamina, and grace.

How really *real*, you may ask, is the imagery technique? Is it only positive thinking combined with idle daydreaming? The answer, still surprising to many, is that imagery has a physical component that can be detected by modern scientific instruments.

Some of the pioneering work in visualization was accomplished by Dr. Richard Swinn of Colorado State University. He began to coach skiers to run their gates mentally, before they even put on their skis. Now imaging has become standard practice in modern slalom, giant slalom, and downhill racing, because it is deemed nearly as important as mastering the techniques of edging, gliding, and the tuck. To understand the dynamics of visualization, researchers have recorded electronically the muscle contractions or, more exactly, the motor-nerve firing sequences that occurred while a rigorous course was run. They then had the skier sit in a laboratory and imagine skiing the course. The firing sequences activated in the actual run were also triggered through imagery, though in more subdued form, of course.

The samurai of feudal Japan were convinced of the value of calm mental preparation for intense physical activity. (They didn't have sensitive monitoring devices, of course.) In fact, samurai spent as much time training their minds as they did their bodies. Two techniques in particular were employed to prepare the mind to be tranquil, fearless, and energetic during combat: breath control and meditation. These warriors spent hours every day honing the disciplines, because they were convinced that the most pernicious threat to their lives was not the external foe but the enemy within—fear. A warrior filled with fear, and thus negative energy, is doomed. Fear inhibits the ability to think quickly or to act fully. Concentration is impossible, though essential; the Ideal Performance State is not present.

The same strategy can be applied to any situation. If a person is afraid, he fails to react optimally. He wastes energy by holding himself back. Fear triumphs.

The samurai warrior practiced meditation and breath control in a private setting. He warded off fear and negative energy, and prepared for the *mon*, the uproar of the clash. It took years to cultivate the right state of calm yet subtle alertness. He focused on the body's fulcrum, the *hara* center (two inches below the navel, where the upper and the lower halves of the body are joined). He strove to maintain a sense of regular and full breathing. In spite of the chaos swirling around him, threatening his very life, the samurai could bring to bear all of his skills and all of his cunning. He issued loud and discordant battle cries that unnerved the enemy. He exhaled at crucial moments.

Japan's legendary swordsman Miyamoto Musashi, the victor in more than sixty mortal contests, recorded his methods in *A Book of Five Rings*, a seventeenth-century work read to this day by martial-arts enthusiasts and businessmen alike. This is how Musashi relates the importance of breath control to the Way of the Sword: "The Body strike means to approach the enemy through a gap in his guard. . . . Approach with the spirit of bouncing the enemy away, striking as strongly as possible in time with your breathing." He details the exhalation of the battle cry: "The three shouts are divided thus: before, during, and after. Shout according to the situation. The voice is a thing of life….In large strategy, at the start of battle we shout as loudly as possible. During the fight, the voice is low-pitched, shouting out as we attack. After the contest, we shout in the wake of our victory." Of crucial importance to the combatant is spiritual bearing. Musashi characterizes it as "determined though calm."

In our research, athletes report optimal performance in a state of calm and subtle alertness. A sense of effortlessness accompanies radical action. There is a heightened feeling of clarity and awareness. The world moves in slow motion. Some athletes—and businesspeople—call this *zoning*. It is an experience that allows a competitive edge to be maintained. Meditation fosters this keenness. When the anxiety of trying to succeed is released, success, calm, and focus come of their own accord.

Basketball players talk about knowing where every player on the court is at any given moment, and which way they may move. The legendary Grand Prix champion Jackie Stewart said that in a race he was aware of the position of every car in relation to his own Formula One. At speeds approaching two hundred miles an hour, he could see individual faces in the crowd. A lapse in concentration could lead to a deadly accident.

Speed skiers—men and women who fly along a specially prepared straight course to see how fast they can go—have spoken of a world that slows down when they hit 114 miles an hour. Individual grains of snow become distinct. All is quiet.

When negative emotions are activated—a tennis player's dread of his opponent's net game, a skier's fear of "the bumps"—the person develops a state quite the opposite of calm, crystalline, slow-motion perception. Fear brings the frantic, panicky feeling that things are out of control, that they are going much too fast, as though the internal VCR were jumping out of gear to fast forward. Such a condition is usually associated with the presence of high-range beta-frequency brain waves, particularly in the dominant hemisphere. Slow, deep breathing induces the effect that leads to the Ideal Performance State.

An emotion associated with top-flight performance is exuberance, joy in action. All outstanding performers participate for the sheer love of the pastime. Enjoyment is the central activating impulse to excellent performance, no matter what the event. Olympic medalist Picabo Street skis hard and fast even when there aren't medals at the end of the run. No tennis player would spend long hours every day of the week, every week of the year, in sweaty practice and trekking all over the world, if he or she didn't really *love* the game. What could appear to be grueling routines are instead, to these people, challenging, exciting, intoxicating opportunities. The Swedish star Bjorn Borg retired from the international tennis circuit when he stopped loving it. Years of much hard work without the continuing sense of fun had taken its toll on the cool Swede. The reward was no longer the game itself, leavened with money and silver platters. Shorn of the passion, Borg felt the effort excessive, and wisely called a halt to tournament play. He had banked millions of dollars, and profitable, enjoyable exhibitions were assured.

We have met many talented athletes with a wide variety of complaints. They may be stuck on a developmental plateau or in a losing streak, or they can't seem to master a weak point in their play. The first question we ask is, "Is it fun anymore?" The answer, more often than not, is, "Fun? How can it be fun? I'm playing miserably and I'm losing all the time."

They think they have to win to have fun. In point of fact, the reverse is true. In professional sports, winning is everything, but it is a long, rocky road to the summit. It is the sense of fun, the enjoyment of the challenge that are sustenance for the competitor along the way. If athletes are going to have fun only when they start winning, they may have to wait a very long time.

Professionals must enjoy the *process* of whatever they commit themselves to. They must establish a sense of delectation in their workouts, runs, and drills. The sense of bliss paves the way for a better performance, even a winning one, because it induces a specific physiological activation involving selective relaxation of muscles and calm and heightened awareness. When one is in a state of tension, irksomeness, ennui, or frustration, no matter what the activity, it's dog's-body work, a bore, a damn chore. Champions don't spring from a mind-set of "I hate to do this."

In this context, it is fascinating how conscious breathing can help a person love what he is doing. Concentrating on breath distracts the mind naturally from all other obsessions, like "Will I win?," "Will I lose?," "What am I doing wrong?," "How did I lose what I had?" Breathing moves consciousness away from critical self-assessment and self-denigration that often tumble about in the mind. Mental status is antithetical to living in the present, to playing each point to the utmost, to relishing every moment of the action. Michael Jordan became a sports legend by playing each and every basketball game as if it were the most important game of the season. He and his Chicago Bulls won a lot of championships.

Fun is indeed so central to performance that it is important for coaches of up-and-coming players to inculcate in them the joy of competition. It's fun to hit the boards. It's terrific to make a shoestring catch. It's a kick to serve an ace. Practice sessions can be made stimulating. *The sense of fun can be cultivated.*

Two of Dr. Loehr's first clients were the Gulliksons, tennis' identical twins, Tom and Tim. Loehr worked first with Tom Gullikson, who wasn't moving up in the computer rankings of the world's top players and needed help to keep his game on track. He was being whipped by players he should have trounced; some of them were just starting out on the professional circuit. Three primary problems were isolated, and coach and player focused on them: Tom's court presence, his low energy during play, his demeanor in response to adversity. Loehr observed Tom on the court with an eye toward emotional and physical reactions, particularly breathing patterns; he observed him walking around on the court between points and while toweling off and sipping water. His observations led to a significant discovery: Tom was holding his breath during play, disrupting the flow of his game; this led to tension, then to erratic play.

Because breathing is an essential medium for maintaining harmony, Loehr began working on Tom's between-points breathing to create an ideal state before each point. He showed Tom how to monitor his own rhythms. When Tom had a hectic exchange that set his heart to pounding, he could calm himself by breathing diaphragmatically—regularly, smoothly, deeply, completely. As he prepared to serve, he elevated his energy level by breathing energetically for maximum oxygenization.

Breathing workouts gave Tom an edge both in energy and in mental state. He was no longer concerning himself with flubbed balls or volleying errors. By focusing his breath just before the point was played, he was in present-centered consciousness. Breath awareness enabled Tom to establish an overall rhythm to his play.

To help Tom coordinate his breathing with his contact points, the word-approach was introduced. Tom began to say "Yesss" when he hit the ball and to issue a long exhalation. In practice, he said it out loud so that Loehr could be certain that Tom's breathing was coordinated. There was a dramatic improvement in all areas of his game. In one year he went from his worst to his best.

Tim Gullikson also had been having trouble on the court. He wasn't reaching his potential, either. His computer ranking was collapsing from a world position of fifteenth in men's singles. On seeing how much his twin's play had improved, Tim put himself under Dr. Loehr's wing as well.

Tim's troubles came from within: he was overly analytical. Every missed shot was dissected. Constant reviewing forced Tim to dwell on the past and look anxiously toward the future. Rarely did it allow him to assume a present-centered state of mind. Tim's way of dealing with his problem was to concentrate on the mechanics. He wanted someone to shift them into gear. Loehr advised Tim that although mechanics were vital, he should not become obsessional about them. In fact, years of training and dedicated work had wrapped Tim in impeccable, technical knowledge. His skills were solid, but he was having trouble accessing them. Freeing up these resources to make them fully available during play became the goal.

Urged to focus on his breath during play, Tim stopped thinking about mechanics. He became present-centered, like a samurai warrior. It is the only state to be in on the playing field—or in the boardroom. (It is ironic that the rational data an athlete works so hard to accumulate— during workouts, in prematch study of an opponent's play, or in the VCR room reviewing one's own performances— must be tuned out of consciousness during play. They must be second nature to him, instinctive, ready for use without his having to call them up.) Tim learned that breathing was a window to his emotional state. Rapid, ragged breathing let him know better than any technical approach when his strategy was out of sync with the reality of the given moment. Breathing techniques could be used to re-establish the right emotional climate and put his body back on automatic.

Tim learned his lesson well, and had an excellent season on the tour. He moved up 112—112!—slots in the computer rankings.

As a doubles team, the Gulliksons improved dramatically, even more than they had in individual play. They reached the doubles finals at Wimbledon before losing to the world's

top-seeded team, the peerless John McEnroe and Peter
Fleming.

Coach Loehr has worked with several women in the top
rankings: Monica Seles, Arantxa Sanchez Vicario, and
Gabriela Sabatini.

Working with amateur athletes, we have discovered serious problems. One woman had developed a condition that
made its appearance every time she played tennis. She became lightheaded to the point of faintness. Severe chest
pains would accompany the lightheadedness and loss of
balance. Often, she would have to quit playing. Fearing a heart
condition, she consulted cardiologists. Treadmill and other
monitoring procedures turned up nothing. Observing her play
a couple of games pinpointed the root of the problem.

Merely walking onto the court created a high-stress situation for the woman. At the beginning of each point she
took a deep breath—and held it. She held her breath as
long as the ball was in play. The longer the point, the more
critical her plight. The moment the point was completed,
she exhaled mightily and panted frantically. As the game
continued, she experienced chest pains and dizziness, as
could have been predicted. The mysterious, crippling habit
of the held breath was so painful that the woman made
errors unconsciously or went for tough winners simply to
get the point over so she could breathe again. After much
concentrated work, she began to breathe as she played, and
to breathe properly. Her dizziness and chest pains vanished,
of course, and they haven't returned.

Bad habits tend to form early in life. We have seen in the
chapter "Breaking the Cycle of Stress" that even children
suffer from stress, and that the competitive atmosphere of
games and matches contributes to that stress. Breath-holding and ragged patterns of breathing are carried into adult
years. Sports are healthy for youngsters, but the children
should not be put "in the fire" until they have been armed

with firefighting tools. Teaching them breath control can help them deal with anger, negativism, tension, and failure.

The age of five or six years is a good time to begin breath training. Youngsters learn quickly, and they find it great fun. It's as though they've been let in on a great big secret—and they have!

Let us present in detail how use of the techniques discussed can breathe vitality into training routines and favorite sports.

Stretching is an indispensable warm-up for any activity as well as for general health. But stretching is a lot more than preparing for play. Stretching slows the aging process. From disuse, from sitting around all day, from general nervous tension, muscles tend to become tight and stiff. Blood flow through muscle tissue is stifled and cells do not get the oxygen they need. Lack of circulation means that waste products are not carried away as swiftly. Many cells will age faster, die faster. We become a garbage dump, prone to disease.

Controlled, directed breathing can set this crippling situation right. Proper breathing stretches the muscles of the chest and diaphragm, making more oxygen available. This action cannot be overly emphasized. Oxygen is the body's vital fuel. When you stretch all of your muscles, blood flow opens up, toxins escape, and nutrients are conveyed effectively to the spots where they can do the most good. Cells are enlivened, cleared up, reoxygenated.

While stretching, use the basic Relaxation Breath. It will help to change the length of contraction at which muscles are set. If you bend to touch your toes and find you can go only partway because your back muscles are "set" at a certain length, breathe deeply, using the Relaxation Breath. The firing of nerve impulses from the brain to the fibers of the muscles slows with the long exhalation. The fibers will release further and you will find yourself stretching farther.

Try this simple experiment. In a standing position, place your hands on your hips. Slowly bend to the right. Imagine yourself breathing into the stretch—into your left neck, side, hip, thigh. Relax. Stretch. Relax. Breathe. Feel your muscles relax as you stretch farther. By overcoming the self-induced tension of your first this-is-my-limit stopping point, you will be able to stretch farther than you thought. Relax. Stretch. Breathe. Relax. Breathe. Slowly stand up straight again and feel the difference between your two sides. To balance the exercise, repeat the stretch to the left.

Understandably, when you stretch to new limits physically as well as emotionally, there may be a bit of pain. If cramping or burning occurs, back off a bit and breathe into the stretch; this allows the muscle to release, and the body should let go of the discomfort. If it doesn't, be cautious. Stop. Stretching must not be done to the point of serious pain. If you feel deep or prolonged pain, you have gone too far. You don't want to injure muscles you are in the process of relaxing.

THE PSYCHOLOGICAL LIFT. When breath is used while stretching, you should be able to go comfortably beyond your limits. It is an exhilarating feeling to be lofted psychologically toward ever greater performance levels. Muscles are achieving their true length rather than their "mental tension length." There will be a buoyancy, a spring, an elasticity in muscles, tendons, and ligaments, reducing the chance of injury. With your muscles at their optimal length, you can maximize performance.

"WARMING DOWN" AFTER PLAY. Breath relaxation and a few stretches help one to integrate the experience and to avoid remaining in either a "keyed up" or a "let down" state. Neither effect is healthy. The use of conscious breathing ushers in a calm, even-energy state.

After physical exertion, it is crucial to ease the body out of its athletic, overextended condition and back into normalcy. All systems—cardiovascular, respiratory, muscular, and nervous—must pass through a transitional phase so that none of them goes into shock: wind down gradually.

SKIING. You know the feeling. It is early in the season and you don't have your ski legs yet. You're on an unfamiliar trail. You turn a corner and there it is. You know it's only a steep pitch, but to your eyes it looks like a cliff bristling with rocks and bare ice and bushes, connected by a few patches of snow. You stop and formulate a plan of action. As you pull up to the lip of the "precipice," your breathing is quick from exertion and fear. You plead with your tightening gut to relax, but it doesn't help. You need another form of coercion. You try a few deep Abdominal Breaths. They work, naturally, Your mind is now calm and you can work out the line of least resistance, the path that avoids obstacles that could damage you or your skis. You prepare for the action so you don't skitter off course at the first mogul. Oxygenate with a few Clavicular (Three-Part) Breaths and then, just before taking off, summon your courage with a couple of Ha! Breaths (silent or outloud). Then go for it!

Skiing can be seen as a kind of paradigm of the relationship between conscious, controlled breathing and rhythmical activity. You navigate the course successfully, getting by that treacherous "precipice." You feel a new kind of rhythm, a rhythm and a pattern of breathing that have evolved spontaneously. You slip into and out of thinking about breath as you slip into and out of the strategies for negotiating the twists and turns. In pure, synchronized motion, you are in a state of exhilaration and pleasure. Accomplished skiers blend intellect, imagination, and physicality, meshing and flowing in continuous, spontaneous motion, zooming down the slope and outlining nature's contours. It is pure accomplishment.

The more you now ski, the quicker and more continuous your skiing will become. There will be fewer times when you will need to stop and analyze difficult situations ahead. You will find yourself skiing confidently into them and through them. Controlled breathing has become a finely tuned strategy, accommodating a rapidly changing environment that throws up potential episodes of stress, danger, physical difficulty, fear, and tension. Your body and your mind and the breathing that links them will have the skill to react positively and enthusiastically to any situation.

Imagine you have run headlong into a mogul. You saw it but chose not to avoid it. In terms of physics, there is the need to absorb shock—a moving object is colliding with a fixed object, a bump. Your legs, torso, and lungs fold to absorb the shock. Your body becomes like an accordion as it pushes air out of your lungs. Coordinated breathing requires that you breathe out. Weight is forced naturally onto the skis's edges, and the exhalation helps you to maintain control. Your ability to accommodate the shock and to turn and prepare for the next bump are accomplished in a single fluid rhythm.

RUNNING. It is a test of the whole person. When you rush through winter's cold, your breathing becomes more effective and pleasant the more you breathe through your nose. True, your oxygen needs will soon be demanding that you breathe through your mouth as well. When you breathe through your nose, the cold air is warmed before it reaches the bronchial tubes and lungs. But cold weather occasionally leads to a runny nose, which can make nasal breathing difficult, if not impossible. There is a solution: blow your nose before you run, while you are running, and when you are through running. Breathing through clear nostrils is a soothing feeling, and it can elevate your mood.

In all seasons, but especially in summer's heat, runners lose a lot of water and electrolytes through the bronchial passages; in fact, more water escapes the body in this way than through perspiration. The passages must stay moist, for water evaporates constantly from their surfaces. Aerobic sports such as running place a high demand on one's internal humidifier. By the time a runner begins to feel dry and thirsty, he or she is already somewhat dehydrated. Slow, even breathing while running will decrease water loss by decreasing dramatically the number of breaths during running or any exercise. The runner should consume adequate fluids about a half hour before setting off, and rehydrate after every workout. Mineral water or natural fruit juice diluted with water is good for rehydrating. Drink often.

All runners have days when they feel they could go on forever. Then there are those days when it's all you can do to finish your favorite loop. Suppose you're still not hitting your stride after a mile or so of warm-up. The Jogging Breath might be just the thing to energize you.

THE JOGGING BREATH

1. Take two quick inhalations through your nose as you run.
2. Exhale forcefully through your mouth, shouting Ha!
   (or it can be silent).
3. Breathe alternately through your nostrils, clearing out mucus.
4. Repeat as needed to rejuvenate.

Coordinate breath and movement. When all is well and the run is exhilarating, the jogger tends not to attend consciously to breath. Coordination of breath and movement is needed to improve performance. Runners who breathe to a count use their steps as a counter and keep breaths in and out. A rhythmic four in, four out or three in, three out is typical. Coming to a hill and need acceleration? Try two in, two out.

WEIGHTLIFTING. Whether you are using weights to train for your sport or lifting weights as a sport in itself, you will find coordination of breath vital to pulling the most from your training. Elemental to breath control is the exhalation during the lift. A smooth exhalation will help you to keep form and motion correct; form is particularly important when hoisting weights, because muscles, tendons, ligaments, and skeletal structure are being loaded with an unusual amount of pressure. Any misalignment—a bent back or a wobbly stance—can cause or exacerbate injury or irritation.

Exhalation on lifting can energize. Energy can be raised to the maximum with a couple of Ha! Breaths before making that final big lift. Oxygenation can be maximized by using the Three-Part or Clavicular Breath; you will start your set of repetitions with a plentiful supply of energy.

There is another reason to exhale through the lifting effort. Pressure in lungs and abdominal cavity will not rise to dangerous levels. Breathing out while lifting also lessens the lifter's chances of developing a hernia. Many weightlifters grunt or yell when they lift. This arouses the lifter to a peak performance. For some, however, a loud noise disrupts concentration. It is a matter of personal preference, as the vocalized exhalation is merely an extension of the silent exhalation.

The importance of concentration while weightlifting cannot be overrated. Anyone who saw the great Alexeyev in action has witnessed awesome powers of concentration. At times the Russian weightlifter seemed to be in a Zen-like meditative state. We do not know what thoughts or internal rhythms the "Russian bear" was keying on, but we know that rhythmic breathing helps to create a meditative state that centers concentration. Use of the breath can help marshal powers and perfect timing to make that big lift possible and safe.

Bodybuilders and weightlifters know the importance of aerobic workouts. In addition, they have specific exercises to increase chest volume and flexibility, not only for strength and looks but for raising the capacity of their lungs. Flexibility is the key. One simple breathing exercise that goes along with such routines is the aforementioned Lung Expander, a marvelous stretch for the chest. Modern lifters, for the most part, avoid becoming "musclebound" because they work stretching into their routines. Breathing into the stretch not only enhances flexibility, it reoxygenates the person for that next set.

A word about pain. We've all heard athletes say "no pain, no gain." The pain referred to is that familiar overall ache and burning sensation in the muscle groups being worked. It is caused by a buildup of lactic acid and should be expected. Other kinds of pain should be suspect. Sharp pains, stabbing pains, joint pains, and feelings of popping or tearing are signals to stop right away and evaluate what is going on. Continued exercise could bring on an injury or worsen an already injured part. Persistent pain should lead to immediate consultation with a trainer or a doctor.

The breathing tactics suggested here apply to all kinds of weightlifting situations, from lifting with free weights to using mechanical apparatus like Nautilus or Universal machines and to exercises such as push-ups or pull-ups in which the weight is that of your own body.

BIKE RIDING. Synchronize breathing with pedaling. Breathe in with six to eight revolutions of the pedals, hold for four pumps, then exhale to eight to ten revolutions. For richer oxygenation while pumping up a hill, don't hold your breath. The Three-Part Breath is helpful in hilly terrain.

TARGET SHOOTING. A slow and smooth exhalation while squeezing the trigger or releasing the arrow will calm nerves, reduce tension, and produce a more accurate shot. *Don't hold your breath.* Use the Centering, or Focusing, Breath. Release it while squeezing or releasing. Think of the arrow, fueled by your concentrated and directed breath, arcing over the landscape. Or of the bullet closing on the bull's-eye.

GOLF. The swing off the tee, like the serve of the tennis ball, requires continuous fluid motion. As you bring the club into the ball, a smooth exhalation and the voicing of a word like "easy" or "smooth" or the humming or singing of a musical phrase helps to eliminate tension and body rigidity—rigidity causes hesitation and hitches. The Relaxation Breath can exorcise basic causes of error in this sport of pinpoint accuracy. (The cup in the green is only four and one-half inches across.) The nervous putter can be calmed with a centered and aligned attitude gained through positive reinforcement of good breathing habits. Imagery can be helpful. Golfers often walk the course before a tournament, shooting imaginary rounds, just as ski racers will slide thoughtfully down a slalom hill and memorize gates and ruts. Visualization rehearsal is preparation for the real thing and eliminates surprises. Use breathing-with-imagery techniques.

WHITEWATER KAYAKING. Obviously, breaths like the Relaxation Breath and the Ha! Breath are useful to prepare the kayaker for the run through challenging rapids. Do not use nose plugs. Some boaters put them on to prevent that annoying water-up-the-nose feeling if they tip over. But inevitably they are lost in difficult situations, such as getting flushed through a class-five waterfall upside down. Flooded nasal passages can add to a panic that could lead to a mistake, such as becoming separated from the boat. Instead of plugs, use a breathing tactic. Practice exhaling while upside down in water. Exhale just enough to keep water from running into your nose. Practice this tactic when you practice your roll and it will become a beneficial habit. The slow exhalation has another benefit. If you hold your breath for more than a short time, carbon dioxide builds up in your lungs, and this leads to an unpleasant sensation of pressure. Slow exhalation releases this pressure and eliminates an annoying distraction.

DANCE. Martha Graham developed the use of breath as one of the foundations of her technique: "The release is the moment in life when you inhale: the breathing going out, when you exhale, is the contraction. It is the first and last moments in life, and it's used as technique, to increase the emotional activity of the body—so that you are teaching the body, not teaching the mind."

WALKING. Although most people don't consider walking a sport, it is the basis of hiking and backpacking, and it is an exercise available to almost all of us. The potential of walking is prodigious. Research has shown that brisk walking 4 or 5 days a week increases aerobic capacity up to 30 percent. It slows or stops osteoporosis, strengthens muscles and the heart, and relaxes nerves. Dr. Migdow walked three miles to and from work for years; he enjoyed the benefits, and felt energized all day! Save your transit fare and walk. Get extra enjoyment from the crisp, sunny day with a walk, not a stroll, in the park. Use the Three-Part Breath for energy when you're lugging your backpack over the pass. Put your imagination to work.

To conclude this chapter, we should like to review, and to amplify, what Coach Loehr in more than two decades as a sports psychologist has learned about mega-performers and peak performances.

Performance consistency is the trademark of all peak performers. Day in and day out, these men and women are able to extend themselves to the upper ranges of talent and skill.

Performance consistency is the fruit of emotional consistency. A peak performer never rides an emotional roller coaster.

Peak performers have developed a unique kind of emotional control—the Ideal Performance State, the emotional balance that makes peak performance possible. It is characterized by feelings of relaxation, calm, and energy— lots of energy, fueled almost exclusively by positive emotions. There may be additional feelings of confidence and optimism.

Peak performers are superb problem solvers. They are superb because they respond emotionally to problems in a unique manner. The "man in the street," when confronted by a stubborn situation, tends to get angry, annoyed, irritated, frustrated; he withdraws energy and commitment; he removes ego from the task; he becomes a bystander. The peak performer triggers in his Ideal Performance State—his I.P.S. He is relaxed, calm, pumped positively, confident, and very much in control. His emotional response is: "I love problems. Give me problems."

To reach one's full potential, to be a crackerjack problem solver—most of us spend our day facing problems—we must take charge of our emotional state. The key to the ultimate control of our complex physiologies is through emotional control.

The key to emotional control is breath control.

Breath control is the ultimate weapon. It is the simplest, safest, cheapest, most accessible handle there is for mastering emotional control, for recharging the Ideal Performance State in response to problems, for staying in control, for becoming a peak performer.

Breath control is the force that leads to the emotional control that leads to the winning feat.

CHAPTER SEVEN

YOUR HEALTH AND DAILY LIFE

Medicine is never simple. Most patients have several diseases and exhibit a multitude of reactions and defenses that are difficult to classify. Never does a given disease look the same in two patients. Experience makes one appreciate the wisdom of Claude Bernard, Walter Cannon,...and Adolph Meyer's view of man as an "infinitely complex psychobiologic unit functioning in relationship to his physical and uniquely social environment." In the broadest sense, disease represents a faulty or inadequate adaptation of the organism to its environment.
—Harrison's *Principles of Internal Medicine*

All too often, many of us consider the issues of health and disease as the exclusive domain of doctors and other health professionals. In fact, they are the products of the interaction of the influences and processes of our daily lives.

Many of us consider the issues of health and disease as the exclusive domain of doctors and other health professionals. In fact, they are the products of the interaction of the influences and processes of our daily lives.

Health is a relative thing; it is not merely the absence of disease. Almost everyone's health could stand improvement. Optimal health is a continually changing puzzle constantly in need of another solution. Health is a state of mental clarity, emotional stability, and physical vitality. It is an integration of all the parts of ourselves with an acceptance of who we are and where we are going. We have the term "holistic health," which means health of the entire organism. A key to true health is breath. Optimal breathing helps us become healthier emotionally and mentally by stimulating release of built-up stress. It helps to overcome physical disease and pain.

Long ago, the medical community was preoccupied with the treatment of disease rather than with the maximizing of health. And for good reason: there was more than enough disease to go around. Health workers were in the position of the man pumping water onto his burning house: he doesn't have time to take out a home-improvement loan. Astonishing twentieth-century advances in the research, treatment, and prevention of disease have given the medical establishment some breathing space to consider the maximization of health potential. Scientific studies to learn the influence of the habits of daily life on health have been conducted. How important has the "daily life" factor turned out to be? Researchers Lee Goldman and Francis Cook of Brigham and Women's Hospital in Boston analyzed 130 reports and studies on cardiac health to assess why there were fewer deaths from coronary artery disease between 1968 and 1976. They concluded that 54 percent of this welcome improvement could be accounted for by lower blood cholesterol and less cigarette smoking. The balance was due principally to improved medical care. Dr. Goldman noted: "The major message to the average American is that you can do more for your own risk of dying from heart disease than your doctor can do for you...." The vast majority of people haven't empowered themselves to do this. Hopefully, breath will be a good first step. Heart-attack deaths have been declining since the 1960s, due to a combination of healthier living habits, better heart medicines, and more intense treatment immediately after a heart attack.

Breathing patterns, relaxation during the day, exercise, and diet lower blood pressure. We already have exhorted you to get at those exercises. Later in this chapter we shall show how breath can be a key to proper diet and to making the best use of the good foods consumed. But first let's review one of the most vital ways in which breath can help you lessen the risk of disease and improve the quality of your life.

SMOKING

If you are a cigarette smoker, quitting is the single most important thing you can do for your health. We have successfully counseled many clients and friends. Breathing is a powerful tool in overcoming nicotine addiction. The reason is simple: smoking is incompatible with deep abdominal breathing. The American Cancer Society recommends breathing exercises as a part of its quitting plan.

To quit smoking, motivation is essential. If one refuses to bury his head in the sand but faces the deadly facts, the strength to quit can be found. The Centers for Disease Control's *Morbidity and Mortality Weekly Report* estimated that 129,000 people would in a year's time die of cancer directly linked to smoking. Sadly, the estimate was borne out. Smoking has been linked not only to lung cancer but to cancer of the larynx, mouth, esophagus, bladder, pancreas, and kidneys. Many smokers die of heart disease before slower-developing cancers begin doing their dirty work. In 1996, 477,000 Americans died of coronary heart disease.

We have detailed the inexorable process of emphysema that affects every smoker to some degree and leaves some of its victims unable to breathe without the help of a machine. Smoking is a leading cause of chronic bronchitis, an unheralded disease that can kill anyone just as dead as cancer can. There is a 20 percent incidence of chronic bronchitis among smokers; there is only a 5 percent incidence among those who have quit smoking. There is a negligible incidence among those who have never smoked.

Chronic bronchitis sufferers have constantly to fight off one bronchial infection after another because their lungs' defense system has been compromised by cigarette smoke. How does this happen? As we have noted, the linings of the bronchial tubes are armed with countless tiny hairs called cilia. When pollution is encountered, the lungs secrete mucus that traps the invading irritants. The cilia wave back and forth to wash the mucus up and out of the lungs, restoring free breathing. The gooey carcinogenic tars found in tobacco smoke, however, are too much even for the stalwart, defending cilia. With each cigarette, tars build up and the cilia slow their waving. Eventually, they come to a dead stop, buried under a mass of tar, dirt, and the other pollution that no longer can be washed out. Bronchial tubes become inflamed, and infective organisms like bacteria and viruses are no longer removed effectively. One damaging result is susceptibility to a variety of infections, some of them life-threatening.

SECOND-HAND SMOKE

Smoking is a punishment that the smoker voluntarily inflicts on himself. But smokers should be aware that they are exposing others to danger. Family, friends, and co-workers are susceptible to "sidestream" smoke, especially in enclosed areas. Nonsmokers exposed to cigarette smoke from co-workers can sustain as much damage to their lungs as if they, themselves, were smoking a pack a day. Evidence of this effect is abundant. The nicotine and carbon monoxide in cigarettes can pass from a pregnant woman into the fetus she carries and cause damage to its brain. Women who smoke have higher rates of miscarriages, stillbirths, and birth defects. Growing children continually exposed to cigarette smoke may be more prone to infections, asthma, and—most important—to becoming smokers themselves. The periodical *Family Practice Recertification* reports that mothers who smoke stunt the development of their non-smoking children's lungs: "The implications are clear for obstructive airways disease in later life." More than 50 million adult Americans smoke, making cigarette smoke the most insidious form of child abuse in our society.

A colleague recounted the sorrowful case of a man who developed lung cancer even though he had never smoked in his life. Unfortunately, he had been in the habit of playing poker several times a week with friends who smoked up a storm in the cardroom. When it was examined in the pathology department of the morgue, the man's lung tissue was found to resemble a smoker's lung tissue.

A patient of ours who quit smoking many years ago continued to suffer bouts of bronchitis several times a year. On inquiry, we were not surprised to learn that there were several heavy smokers in the office where she worked. She has had no recurrence of the bronchitis since leaving that job.

"Light" cigarettes seem not to be a solution to the smoking problem. If Dr. Neal L. Benowitz and his colleagues at the University of California are right, "light" cigarettes are a deadly illusion. Their survey of 272 volunteers turned up no relationship between Federal Trade Commission ratings of the brands smoked and the amount of nicotine absorbed by the volunteers. The commission's analytical machines smoked each brand at the same steady, impartial rate. Dr. Benowitz found that humans smoking "light" cigarettes tend to inhale more frequently and deeply and to light up more often. Also, the unfiltered sidestream smoke from the "safer" light brands is just as bad as that from "stronger" brands; the smoker and those around him get about the same levels of tar, nicotine, and deadly carbon monoxide.

CARBON MONOXIDE

A less publicized though equally poisonous product of tobacco smoke is carbon monoxide. It originates in the partial burning of some paper or tobacco. Instead of combining with two oxygen atoms to produce carbon dioxide, the carbon atom combines with only one. The result is a gas that combines "avidly" (as medical texts say) with the hemoglobin in red blood cells. When this happens, each affected hemoglobin molecule becomes totally useless; oxygen is blocked out of its rightful place in the transport process. Worse, the carbon monoxide stays put, because it sticks to the hemoglobin more energetically than does oxygen or carbon dioxide. Small amounts of carbon monoxide bring on drowsiness, confusion, and decreased performance; higher levels cause brain damage, heart attack, and fatal anoxia.

The ironic twist of carbon monoxide's effect on a smoker is that the breathless feeling it induces makes him want to breathe faster. But no matter how fast he puffs and gasps, it is to no avail. The oxygen-carrying capacity of the blood has been crippled; all that extra oxygen gulped in is merely exhaled without being absorbed. It takes a long time to restore comfortable oxygen levels.

Auto exhaust is a major source of carbon monoxide. Each day, millions of particles of carbon monoxide (CO) are spewed into the atmosphere by the cars we drive. Most of them soar into the atmosphere. However, if you live in a city and walk around, or if you live near busy roadways, a small percentage of CO will get into your bloodstream.

It is imperative for optimal health performance to do what you can to stop smoking. Car pool if you can. Use public transportation. Help cut down on the CO.

STROKE

The brain, as we all know, has a tremendous appetite for oxygen. By decreasing cerebral blood flow, smoking acts directly to deprive the brain of oxygen. Stroke can be provoked. In an article in the *Journal of the American Medical Association*, researchers reported that they had found lower blood flow to the gray matter of the brain in smokers than in nonsmokers. Smoking brought about this anomaly "probably by enhancing cerebral arteriosclerosis," that is, by the hardening and narrowing of the arteries that feed the brain: "Cigarette smoking should be considered as a risk factor related to increased incidence of stroke as well as for enhanced cerebral arteriosclerosis."

POLONIUM

With polonium we have reached the end of the morbid litany of smokers' ills, and what an end it is. Writing in the *New England Journal of Medicine*, Dr. R. T. Ravenholt revealed that tobacco smoke is the most dangerous source of radiation exposure to the average American. The culprits are microscopic particles of radioactive polonium. These particles, with the smoke, enter the body and settle in the bronchial tubes. They become absorbed into the tissues and the bloodstream. Once in circulation, they can lodge anywhere in the body and produce malignant growths.

THE ROAD BACK

If you are a smoker, we hope we have provided you with the motivation for never buying another pack. Simply visualizing all that dry ash and those harsh, invasive chemicals ruining moist and delicate lungs helps many people keep to their pledge to stop. At present, there are many natural techniques helping people to stop smoking. They include homeopathic remedies, acupuncture, and herbal detoxification. There are patches and drugs. Your physician can suggest appropriate therapies. The American Cancer Society has a free seven-day program. Some individuals choose to taper off over a longer period of time. Still others find it easier to quit "cold turkey." Whichever path you choose, keep in mind that your body is a hundred percent behind your efforts to stop smoking. Your body *wants* to repair itself, it *wants* to be healthy again. Two-packs-a-day smokers can return to normal respiratory function. Even smokers who have been hospitalized for emphysema can expect relief from respiratory distress if they successfully swear off smoking forever. This is one man's story:

He smoked like a chimney in high school and in college, where he majored in English. The pressure of examinations, term papers, and the academic grind caused him to rely more and more on the nicotine habit. Eventually, he was up to forty cigarettes a day. (That's $1,200 a year for cigarettes!) One day, he was telling a friend about his efforts to improve his stamina in skiing, his favorite sport; he was an avid downhiller. The friend mentioned his experience with the beneficial by-products of running. The heavy smoker decided to give it a try. He didn't do well at first, of course; his smoking habit cut into his wind, though he was still a youth. But he persisted, and presently he noticed that the more often he ran, the less he liked to smoke. He found himself smoking only a few cigarettes per day, and running ever-greater distances. One day, he realized that even one cigarette could make him a bit dizzy and likely to cough. His body was returning to the healthy state it had been in before he put a match to his first cigarette. The running was training his lungs to breathe deeper and to flex more easily, and he was now dependent on the gusts of fresh oxygen that running gave him. He became addicted to health. He dropped the smoking habit forever. Ten years later, after a physical, he was told by his doctor that he had recorded the highest lung capacity of all the doctor's patients.

THE CLEANSING PROCESS

One problem that smokers may encounter when they quit is, paradoxically, a seeming increase in their "smoker's cough." This is because their lungs, no longer beaten into submission by a barrage of toxic waste, are attempting to loosen and clear themselves of many years' accumulation of crud. At first, the cough is the body's only remaining defense. But as mucus is cleared, the cells that produce the cilia will "get back on their feet" or be replaced. The automatic process of clearing the bronchial tubes resumes. To facilitate the getting-healthier process, the Cleansing Breath can be practiced. Kapalabhati and Ha! Breathing help to clear the lungs. The Lung Expander restores flexibility of lungs and chest. The Lung Strengthener is excellent for former smokers in self-repair, and for asthma sufferers.

Anyone who has quit smoking can confirm that it is perfectly natural to experience cravings for a cigarette. This old habit dies hard, very hard. The cravings are a form of stress. But now you know how to deflect stress. Instead of lighting up, you go into deep abdominal breathing. You inhale fresh, clean air instead of smoke. You relax any tension.

To vanquish any craving, try a simple variant of the basic Abdominal Breath: Ujjai, or the Whooshing Breath. Ujjai means "that which leads to victory." In this case, it is victory over the smoking habit.

UJJAI: THE WHOOSHING BREATH

1. Sit comfortably and loosen any constricting garments—collars, ties, belts, and the like. Make sure your nostrils are clear. Do a few rounds of Kapalabhati. Blow your nose if necessary.
2. Do the Abdominal Breath, but flare your nostrils and inhale through your nose. Make a whooshing sound at the back of your throat.
3. Exhale through your nose, making the same whooshing sound. (Done correctly, it sounds like breaking ocean waves.)
4. Repeat Steps 2 and 3 five to ten times.

Ujjai creates a stronger air flow and clears your lungs of impurities. As you do it, you will become acutely aware of your respiratory system: flared nostrils, throat, lung expansion. You will feel the progress you are making on the return road to maximizing your pulmonary potential. *This kind of awareness is the cornerstone of breathing techniques.* (Vitamins, too, can be helpful in healing lungs. Vitamins A, C, and E are said to speed repair of bronchial tubes, mucous membranes, and alveoli.)

BLOOD PRESSURE

Any relaxing type of breath helps to control and reduce high blood pressure. This is especially good news for those who, because of a history of heart disease or the like, should not employ the breath-holding tactic introduced earlier. Use of breath in a relaxing mode is safe and harmless, and it can be a key element in any program to reduce or eliminate the use of drugs. The National Heart, Lung, and Blood Institute states that in cases of mild hypertension, nondrug therapies should be "pursued aggressively." It also recommends that diet, exercise, and behavior modification be employed in conjunction with drug treatment of more severe cases.

Many pressure-reducing drugs have unpleasant side effects. Some may be damaging. Any tactic to avoid them is worthwhile. Sixty million Americans have some form of high blood pressure, and the incidence of the disease seems to be accelerating in the Western industrialized nations. Many of the factors contributing to high blood pressure have been implicated as unhealthy in other ways: high cholesterol, obesity, lack of exercise, overreaction to stress, and, of course, smoking.

The mechanics of high blood pressure work in two ways. The first is the high resting tone or spasm of the muscles controlling the blood vessels. The second is a buildup of fatty chemicals on the inner walls of the vessels. This buildup, called arterial plaque, stiffens and fills the vessels, crippling their ability to swell or slacken to accommodate varying blood flow and to reduce blood flow itself. The ability to relax and respond calmly to excruciating stresses in modern life is crucial to an effective nondrug approach to high blood pressure. Abdominal Breath for relaxation can provide a key aid. Many health workers and researchers support this view. Dr. Robert S. Eliot, who suffered a heart attack at the age of forty-four, describes people who respond to stress with cardiovascular distress as "hot reactors." He found that 20 percent of healthy people respond to mental tasks, such as arithmetic, either by increasing their heart rate disproportionately or by increasing their heart rate and constricting their blood vessels. The strain is enormous. It is like driving fifty-five miles per hour in second gear. Just around the bend are transient high blood pressure, stroke, and heart attack. Not surprisingly, one of Dr. Eliot's primary recommendations is to relax. He recommends abdominal breathing for ten to fifteen minutes with creative imagery of, say, a beautiful beach or a favorite vacation spot. The combination should release internal tension and reduce overreaction of the heart and blood vessels, thus modifying the risk of heart attack, heart disease, and stroke. The Menninger Foundation, in Kansas, uses relaxation techniques employing deep breathing and biofeedback apparatus that monitors finger temperature; a rise in temperature indicates a deep state of relaxation. Through these techniques, 90 percent of the foundation's high blood pressure patients shift their pressure to a normal range.

Another researcher, Dr. Herbert Benson, of Boston's Beth Israel Hospital, reports gratifying results with relaxation methods that include breathing techniques. He tells subjects: "Breathe through your nose. Become aware of your breathing. As you exhale, say the word 'one' silently to yourself." Any word, even your own name, can be used to focus consciousness. Try the word *Om*, the universal sound whose gentle vibration is itself a relaxer. Dr. Benson's investigations "demonstrate that regular elicitation of the relaxation response lowers blood pressure in both untreated and pharmacologically treated hypertensive patients."

Another investigator, Dr. Chandra Patel, of London, reduced a patient's blood pressure by using biofeedback in conjunction with relaxation techniques. He employed a machine that measured the activity of the sympathetic nervous system indirectly through changes in the skin's electrical resistance. It let the patient know when the relaxation technique was successful, thus acting as a guide to blood pressure reduction. Breathing, Dr. Patel observed, was of central importance in therapy: "The patients were asked to pay attention to their breathing…They found it difficult to forget their breathing movements; they used them as the object for their concentration." A follow-up study showed that many patients retained the beneficial effects of the program a year later.

W. Stewart Agras, of Stanford University, used relaxation techniques that included deep breathing without biofeedback: "Clearly, we have a procedure that works—it can significantly lower blood pressure, provide additional benefits to drug treatment, and it doesn't require the elaborate apparatus required for biofeedback."

With the use of deep, slow, rhythmic breathing you can reduce blood pressure at no expense and in the privacy of your own home—no need for machines. In our experience, a simple five-minute relaxation-breathing session can lower blood pressure by twenty to thirty points of systolic pressure (that is, when the heart is contracting) and ten to fifteen points of diastolic pressure (when the heart is relaxing). We have found, as has Dr. Agras, that when relaxation is practiced twice daily, blood pressure tends to stay down during the entire day. We have helped people forgo their blood pressure medication, thanks to the success of breathing techniques. The effect of relaxation breathing can be enhanced by the use of gentle music and through mental imagery focused on the circulatory system.

We must emphasize that it takes time for breathing techniques to lower blood pressure. The model of exercise is appropriate here. Anyone who has exercised over a prolonged period understands the gradual process of building up endurance and losing weight. The same thing occurs with the positive results of deep breathing and relaxation techniques—but invisibly. "All" you get is a feeling—a feeling of life, energy, and radiance. The glow of health always comes from within.

Here is how one woman, through the use of breath techniques, improved both her blood pressure and her outlook on life.

She was thirty-nine years old and taught gym classes in a school in a suburb of a large east-coast city. Her doctor informed her that she had hypertension (high blood pressure). Together, they worked to find an appropriate medication. After trying many drugs, she was finally able to moderate her pressure, but she still wasn't satisfied. When she heard about breathing techniques, she decided to give them a try. Using her breath, she reached a relaxed state that enabled her to express the stress and tensions in her life. It may seem paradoxical to speak of stress and relaxation in the same breath, but it indeed makes sense. It is like the gardener who loosens the soil before pulling the weeds. When he does, the weeds come out, roots and all. If tensions are expressed while one is in a tense mode, it is like snapping off weeds at ground level. The real problems—the roots—remain buried. By being able to bring underlying tensions to the surface while engaged in relaxation breathing, the woman was able to reduce the levels of the medication she had depended on to control her blood pressure.

(Breathing tactics intended to work on blood pressure are adjuncts to any necessary professional medical attention. *Check with your doctor.* He or she is the sole judge as to when you may be able to reduce any medication.)

OVEREATING

Overeating and obesity are an epidemic disease. Just look around you. Anyone 20 percent or more overweight is obese, according to the National Institutes of Health. An NIH panel chairman, Jules Hirsch, said, "Obesity is a killer...It is a killer as smoking is." This killer is stalking an estimated 45 million Americans. Every pound of excess fat puts an additional load on the heart. Obesity increases the risk of diabetes, cancer, high cholesterol, and hypertension.

Nobody wants to be fat. Most of us rarely "pig out." But neither do most of us eat properly. In many cases the problem with the typical American diet isn't so much a matter of the *amount* we eat as *what* we eat and *how* we eat it.

Examine your eating patterns. When do you eat? What motivates you to eat? We all know a person who reacts to a dreadful day not by talking openly to a loved one, not by

exercising to release pent-up anxiety and attendant toxins
that have built up hour by hour, but by staging a lightning
commando raid on the refrigerator and the cupboard.
When he reaches impulsively for those snacks, he is not
likely to come up with a spear of raw broccoli vinaigrette.
He goes for the jelly donuts, ice cream, and potato chips.
Why does he snack in such a pattern? Why does he even
buy the foods he does? The answers can be found in inter-
twined psychological and physiological processes.

With our earliest experiences in infancy, food was established as the original expression of love. When an adult
needs to feel comforted, food is a natural, although regres-
sive, comfort to turn to. Sugary foods are picked for reactive
snacks because sugar is sweet. The message gets reinforced.
The feeling of comfort isn't simply psychological. Eating
signals the pituitary to release beta-endorphins, the same
chemicals that put a brake on the fight-or-flight response.
The purpose of endorphin release in this instance is to slow
and smooth out the digestive process. Nerve receptors in
the gut respond to endorphins just as they do to opiates
administered from outside. They keep digestion efficient.
Food addiction is possible because of the pleasure that beta-
endorphins provide.

How can the pattern be broken? Well, slow, deep,
rhythmic breathing triggers the release of endorphins.
After a frustrating day at the job, the relaxing Abdominal
Breath can be practiced *before* rushing to the "food solution" to distress. The reactive eating response may be
avoided entirely. Even if a snack is consumed, a little
"breathing space" has been created in which the kind of
food to be eaten later can be plotted. Fruit is a good
choice—no cholesterol and plenty of vitamins and
minerals—and it's so much healthier than sweets and
pastries, which provide only "empty" calories. Raw vegetables are a good choice as well. Fruit and vegetables

provide a healthy alternative to fatty foods, which accelerate the process of arteriosclerosis, the clogging of the
arteries with plaque, whose key constituent is cholesterol.

Breathing techniques help you digest food during main
meals as well as temper your appetite, and you will enjoy
the meal more. Directed breathing relaxes you before you
go to the table. It puts you in the proper state of mind. The
glands in your mouth can produce two kinds of saliva.
When the diner is relaxed and ready to eat, the parotid
glands produce saliva that contains digestive enzymes and is
watery; it easily dissolves food being chewed. Under stress,
however, the sublingual glands exude a thick saliva that is
devoid of digestive enzymes. Clearly, relaxing before a meal
is the first step toward ease of digestion. Directed breathing
helps in chewing food thoroughly; it helps to get the most
out of each morsel. Well-chewed food is easier to digest. By
timing chews with breath in a meditative manner, a relaxed
mood can be preserved throughout the entire meal. Digestion and disposition are closely linked.

For those trying to lose weight and for those who suffer
from indigestion, this breath technique can be a godsend:

THE ENJOY YOUR-MEAL BREATH

1. Execute a few Ha! Breaths to stimulate appetite and the
   digestive organs before the meal.
2. Do a minute or two of the Abdominal Breath to induce
   relaxation.
3. Start to eat. As you chew the first mouthful, inhale
   through your nose for four chews.
4. Hold for four chews. (If you have a history of heart
   disease, stroke, or very high blood pressure, skip this step.)
5. Exhale for four chews.
6. Do three rounds of Steps 3 to 5 for full chewing of each
   mouthful.

(*Warning:* Be careful not to "inhale" your food as you

breathe through your nose. It can ruin digestion and
cause considerable discomfort.) Chew slowly so that
your breath is slow. Do it with awareness of the taste
and texture of the food.

Eating less through directed breathing leads to easier
breathing, because body fat in the abdominal region is
being trimmed. Fat deposits crowd the diaphragm, impede
flexibility, and keep the lungs from opening up as fully as
possible. The overweight person has to breathe more often
to get a sufficient amount of air, but he breathes easier
with every pound lost. Presently, he will be able to bend
over and put on his shoes and tie the laces without gasp-
ing for air.

CONSTIPATION

Millions of men and women in our society suffer from
constipation.

When one is constipated, food—especially protein—sits in
the colon and putrefies. Because food that the system has difficulty digesting is frequently wolfed down and overeaten—
rich and fatty foods in particular—meals are not fully digested
and assimilated. Unfriendly bacteria and fungi move in and
begin to use the morsels as their own nourishment. They
eliminate *their* waste products in the person's intestines as if
they were a cesspool. This waste enters the bloodstream,
and constipation worsens. Ammonia, which affects the
liver and even a person's concentration, is produced. Various precarcinogenic nitrols and nitrosides are generated.
Chemicals such as indols are produced. They all foul the
nervous system and render the colon even more sluggish.

There is, of course, a way to improve the elimination
process directly. That old standby, the ancient breath
process called Kapalabhati, stimulates the digestive system
to start up again and function efficiently. Let's review the
"skull cleanser" in relation to the organs of digestion:

KAPALABHATI (A REPRISE)

1. Get comfortable in a sitting position.
2. Do one or two minutes of the Abdominal Breath and
   the Relaxation Breath.
3. Inhale fully.
4. Expel short, forceful exhalations through the left
   nostril while pulling in your abdomen with each
   exhalation. You will experience a staccato exhalation
   until your lungs are fully emptied.
5. Repeat full inhalations and staccato exhalations ten
   times. Any inhalation that takes place between
   staccato exhalations should be entirely involuntary.
6. Inhale fully.
7. Exhale fully.
8. Breathe in three-quarters capacity of your lungs and
   hold it as long as comfortable, then exhale.
9. Repeat Steps 4–8 through the right nostril.
10. Repeat Steps 4–8 through both nostrils simultaneously.
    (If you have a history of high blood pressure, heart
    disease, or stroke, release the breath slowly instead of
    holding it. A person with epilepsy should *never* deep-
    breathe rapidly.)

When you pull in your abdomen with each short exhalation, you establish a rhythm: in quick succession compress,
release, compress, release, compress, release. It is like internal jogging. It gets the circulation going throughout the
digestive tract and physically stimulates the motion of the
gut. Your system "wakes up" and does its job. At first, you
may do only five to ten short exhalations per breath. Over a
period of time you will want to do as many as a hundred.

If you feel you're "in trouble" after ten exhalations, take a
deep breath and breathe out fully. Then inhale to two-thirds
of capacity and hold the breath as long as it is comfortable.
Exhale. Resume normal breathing, or repeat the technique.

No matter how many exhalations you do, always end in the same way to derive the most benefit from the technique.

Taking a deep breath in and out gives an extra pump to the abdomen. It cleans out the lungs so efficiently that when only a two-thirds breath is taken, tremendous oxygenation revitalizing the whole system is experienced. Breathing in only two-thirds of capacity avoids hyperventilation and the reaction of a low blood pressure.

If you think Kapalabhati is not appropriate, there is an alternative technique that accomplishes similar effects. It is called the Stomach-Pump Breath, or Abdominal Lift. It derives from the basic Abdominal Breath.

THE STOMACH-PUMP BREATH (ABDOMINAL LIFT)

1. Stand up.
2. Take a deep breath, then exhale all of it.
3. Raise your arms straight up and inhale.
4. Exhale fully while lowering yourself smoothly to the squatting position, hands on knees, head down.
5. Move your abdomen in and out as you complete exhaling—as if it were a pump.
6. Repeat several times, as you feel like it.

Doing the Stomach-Pump Breath first thing in the morning will help generate a bowel movement. It will also stimulate appetite and digestive juices.

A discussion of this area of stress is not complete without mentioning hemorrhoids, those distended anal blood vessels which are the scourge of millions. Years of straining in a position not optimal for bowel movement (the best position anatomically is the squatting position) leads to a strain on the anal muscles and vessels, which eventually distend like a balloon. The result: pain, an increased difficulty in the movement of bowels, sometimes bleeding. Through a combination of appropriate breathing techniques, a diet high in fiber foods such as fruits, vegetables, and whole grains, and a reduction in foods that reinforce constipation (such as sugar, white flour products, and fried, fatty foods), hemorrhoids as well as constipation can be alleviated, even prevented. Avoid coffee and caffeine. They invariably aggravate hemorrhoids. For quick relief, try rubbing witch hazel on the hemorrhoids after each movement; it helps to shrink the blood vessels. Nature *does* provide!

HEADACHE RELIEF

Headaches are a health problem as common as constipation. Many Americans even accept them as a part of everyday life. But there is good news. While the possibility of having a headache cannot be eliminated, the pain of many headaches can be reduced by the use of breath technique in conjunction with other relaxation techniques.

A businesswoman had a history of migraine and tension headaches. She used breath technique and the relaxation imagery of the cool, restful scene of her seashore home. The combination helped her achieve a 50 percent reduction in the number of attacks.

Another woman was experiencing intense headaches, constipation, shoulder pain, and sciatica. The symptoms were largely relieved through the practice of easy stress-reduction techniques—the simple, basic Abdominal Breath was one, the Alternate Nostril Breath a second. She deflects potential headaches with five minutes of the Alternate Nostril Breath on rising in the morning. Any headache that comes during the workday remains at a manageable level and goes away rather quickly. If it recurs, it is not severe. Her constipation cleared up. Through Kapalabhati she has reduced stress in the abdominal area. When she feels tension in her shoulders, she goes to the Relaxation Breath. Her shoulders relax, pain vanishes. There has been a pleasurable side effect: she has become more aware of her body.

PAIN CONTROL

Breathing tactics can be applied to pain in many situations. The successful use of breathing for pain control in childbirth has long been established, yet many people unfortunately remain ignorant of this personal source of relief for day-to-day pain.

Pain has a purpose. Its message is ignored at peril. It is important to gain an understanding of pain, especially its source, as one works to relieving it.

Chronic pain, severe or persistent, requires professional consultation before a successful program of management begins.

Relaxation techniques have become a vital component of pain management. Dr. C. Norman Shealy, a specialist in pain research and relaxation, agrees that "all good relaxation techniques begin with voluntary deep breathing. It sends a signal to the autonomic nervous system that relaxation is about to occur."

Focusing on breath usually takes the mind off pain. In addition to the change in attention, breath enables the sufferer to relax muscles in the vicinity of pain. This is especially important when pain is experienced; muscles in the affected area tend to contract and become rigid. The stiffness resulting in, say, an injured joint has its adaptive side. It keeps the joint from being used easily. The same rigidity restricts the flow of blood and lymphatic fluid through the area. This slows the supply of healing agents and the removal of damaged tissue. Breathing for relaxation opens up the flow and speeds healing.

The use of breathing techniques for alleviating pain has gained acceptance in the medical community. An emergency-room study with follow-up discovered that patients healed up to three times faster and pain diminished when injury was followed by deep breathing exercises and simultaneous review of the event of the injury; emotions and pain of the incident are thus released consciously.

Dr. Gerald M. Arohoff, director of the Boston Pain Center at Spaulding Rehabilitation Hospital, uses deep breathing as part of the systematic relaxation training of his chronic pain-management program. He has commented, "The method is particularly useful because the results are felt immediately by the patient and it is something they can learn to do by themselves for pain control." In fact, almost all clinics use breathing techniques as part of their pain-management program.

For the control of pain, as well as for general relaxation, deep abdominal breathing works best if one is in the habit of doing the Relaxation Breath every day. The response to pain becomes automatic. Dr. Donald Pentecost, of Fort Worth, Texas, teaches deep abdominal breathing to his patients *before* they undergo surgery. "Afterwards," he told us, "they may be in too much pain and not as receptive. Yet I have found that if they learn the technique in advance and start breathing that way in the recovery room, they usually require less medication because they are in less pain postoperatively." This is preventive medicine at its best.

The following breath technique is designed to be used with imagery to release pain such as headaches, menstrual cramps, and back pain. It is best done at a time of day when you have fifteen to twenty minutes to yourself in a relaxed setting. As with any relaxing technique, loosen any restrictive clothing.

THE RELIEVING-OR-RELEASING-PAIN-WITH-IMAGERY BREATH

1. Keep your eyes closed throughout.
2. Begin abdominal breathing.
3. Imagine tension leaving your body, like a vapor or a stream of color, with each exhalation.

4. Imagine relaxation coming in with each inhalation.
5. Move parts of your body as you breathe, if it helps to release any general tension.
6. Imagine your incoming breath traveling to the area of pain and filling it with calmness.
7. Imagine the pain flowing out with each exhalation.
8. Allow yourself, through crying or sighing, to release any emotion related to the pain.
9. Continue Steps 5 through 8 for five to ten minutes.
10. Feel the movement of your breath again.
11. Stretch your arms and legs.
12. Open your eyes when you feel better.

Practice this technique when you do not have pain; if pain comes, you can easily shift into the relaxation pain-releasing mode.

INJURIES

The use of imagery, as in the pain-control breath above, can be extended to ease many health problems.

Even if not serious, an injury can be painful, and it can limit movement and activity. Because the use of imagery shortens healing time, the use of breath coupled with imagery allows the injured person to resume an active life sooner.

When mental images are used to reach the source of an injury, this must be done with self-compassion—nonjudgmentally, as it were. Be with the part, simply, openly, acceptingly. Breathe deeply and imagine breath's energy going directly to the afflicted area—as if breath were iron filings and the strain of the wrench or the tear were a magnet. Perceive the energy going there in the form of light.

The pain-control breath is a handy way to move into imagery for injury-healing. Begin the breath as usual, but when you reach Step 8—"Allow yourself, through crying or sighing, to release any emotion related to the pain"—go

back in mind to the time that the injury occurred. What
happened? What were the stresses? What were your immediate thoughts? Allow yourself to re-experience the emotions. Play back—as if in slow motion—the mental "film"
of the injury. You were running and fell. You tripped on
something. You banged your head. Whatever happened,
you may never have fully experienced your anger, grief, or
rage. Do so now. Clean out your system. If you have to
curse, *curse!* If you feel sadness or depression or fury at yourself, that's okay, too. You may find yourself crying as the
tensions begin to boil up, as you experience the core feelings and then release them.

After you have completed the initial emotional cleansing, it is valuable to go back and in your mind once more
replay the accident, now with the benefit of a clear head
and consciousness. Look for clues as to why the accident
happened. Was it linked to an emotion? To a snit, say, or to
depression? It has been proven statistically that people have
accidents most often when they are depressed. In the accident itself and in its aftermath, many feelings surge forth.
Everybody has seen (or heard of) a person who hurt himself
by bumping into an inanimate object and then, in a rage,
punched or kicked the object, further injuring himself. Professional basketball's foremost scorer, Kareem Abdul-Jabbar,
was once elbowed in the eye. In the moments after the
dizzying blow, he fired up his rage to such intensity that he
slammed a fist into a metal upright of the backboard as hard
as he could, shattering bones in the hand. "It was the stu-
pidest thing I have ever done," he announced after being
sidelined for more than a month.

Replaying an accident can assist the victim in reaching
and releasing the emotions surrounding the injury, in physical and psychological senses, thereby reducing the chance
that the injury could happen again.

CONVALESCENCE

The pain-control breath is used in the process of recovery from disease. With one exception, the process is the same: instead of replaying an injury, you review the experience of becoming ill and coming to terms with disease. Frequently, powerful emotions are touched off by the realization that a serious illness is present. Fear, rage, self-pity (Why me?), and envy are a few of the emotions that might be bound up with the experience of illness. Understandably, their release through breathing aids the recovery process.

Serious illness brings on a great deal of stress. Apart from worry over his health, a patient may be subjected to impersonal hospital routine, frequent medical tests, invasive diagnostic procedures, surgery, and harsh but necessary medications like chemotherapy or intravenous antibiotics. In the face of all of these foreign procedures, the patient is expected to keep up a peppy mental attitude, to be a "fighter," to keep his old chin up. Relaxation techniques speed healing, because the immune system and the healing process are crippled by stress; whatever counteracts stress benefits the recovering patient.

Any breathing exercise for relaxation helps to counter stress. The Alternate Nostril Breath is an especially potent defense against both worry and stress. It quickly acts to clear the mind and relax mental as well as physical tension. Laughter is a wonderful healer, as we've said, so long as it doesn't hurt when you laugh.

IMAGING FOR MAXIMIZING HEALTH

The use of imagery with breathing is an excellent technique for convalescence. It is also an excellent technique for maximizing general health and healing. As we combine relaxation with imagery, we calm nerves, strengthen the immune system, and maximize respiration, circulation, and digestion. We also focus the body's healing capacity on a particular area. Dr. Migdow has seen patients heal polyps, cysts, eye infections, tumors, thyroid disease, and high blood pressure through visualization. Imagery can be brought into play in dealing with minor annoyances like aches or pains of the common cold or a charley horse after a strenuous workout. There are imagery techniques for different parts of the body. Variations on basic themes or very personal imagery can be created.

As the imager feels relaxation settling in, he should think about his entire body, area by area, becoming keenly aware of how each part feels, finding areas of tension concealed during the busy day. Where attention must be paid, images can focus healing energy and compassion on the afflicted part.

THE HEAD

The head is often subject to a variety of aches, pains, and feelings of fatigue and stuffiness. We have found that one of the most helpful images for "curing" the head is the sea—the rolling, healing ocean continuously washing over the delicate brain. In reality, the brain is bathed in cerebrospinal fluid with a chemical composition not unlike that of sea water; the image is especially apt.

Eye-aches are a common problem. Usually, they can be remedied by the simple therapy of a firm massage with fingertips at the exact center of each temple. It is even better if you can have someone do this to you while you concentrate wholly on the relaxing and healthy visualization of images. Remember the sea.

Your brain is the crown of your "body tree." It should be beneficial if you image your brain as that. As your temples are being massaged, breathe deeply and feel your spine lengthen and your lungs expand. The spine will roll up and down like the marvelously flexible tail of a sea horse, and the lungs will fill the chest with ease.

Tension and pain in the head, neck, or back are caused sometimes by jaw tension. For their weight, jaw muscles are the strongest muscles in the body. If you've ever been bitten, you know firsthand that this is so. When burdened with overwhelming tension, many people clench their jaws. This is part of the scream response seen in many animals when they are being attacked or are on the attack. When most people are attacked, especially psychologically, they tend to set off the physiological fight-or-flight mechanism and the scream response. Because screaming is not socially acceptable (usually), any yell is restrained or aborted, and the jaw tightens a bit more. With the accumulation of tension, people suffer tooth-grinding, periodontal disease, headache, and backache.

If clenched jaw is a problem, it is a good idea to spend a few minutes every day massaging the jaw muscles. The massage might even bring up some emotional pain. Good! Better out than in! Breathe in a relaxing mode. Imagine the pain dissolving into a river of light and flowing out of the jaw. A friend of ours who had some trouble with tooth-grinding found this simple technique pleasant and relaxing. He will eliminate the problem completely.

Tensions in the neck are often difficult to release. Breathing and the right imaging can be of service here, too. The neck is essentially the collar for the head. If you have had a shirt whose collar you outgrew, that pinched you when you buttoned it or tried to button it, you know what a tight neck is. Mentally unbutton that tight collar. Breathe out tension, inhale calmness and relaxation, stretch your neck.

One easy, loosening exercise that combines abdominal breathing with gentle stretch and imagery is what we call the Numbers Game.

1. Start deep abdominal breathing while imagining the very top of your head to be the tip of a pen.

2. Use that imaginary pen to write carefully the numbers from one to ten on an imaginary surface in your head. Move the pen gently, but use the full range of motion to write nice, big numbers in an even manner.

THE CHEST

Maximum chest inflation is not needed most of the time. Daily life is not a bodybuilding contest or a military parade. The bantam-rooster look is the physical counterpart of an overinflated ego. Except in circumstances in which one-hundred-percent oxygenation is needed (see the Three-Part Breath), this look can be avoided.

In proper relaxed breathing, the chest expands—automatically. It happens when a deep, relaxed abdominal breath is taken. The lower back and even the shoulder blades expand a bit, because ribs extend around the back. As the lower lungs fill, the back ribs expand. An appropriate image for this process is one of soft but strong angel's wings expanding with each inhalation. It is relaxing to accentuate this expansion gently. When a person breathes fully from time to time during the day, making his chest expand and respiratory muscles work effectively, he begins to breathe fully all the time.

THE ABDOMEN

Deep breathing in the abdominal area helps to loosen blocked and impacted food in the bowels. It spurs digestion. It provides a healthy tone. The abdominal organs are the center of the body's food operations and must be treated responsibly if they are to give long and faithful service. One of the common conditions of advanced age is diverticulosis. It is often caused by the lack of dietary fiber; the intestines lose muscular tone and become flabby and weak. Food becomes caught in a sac (pocket) of the intestines. It sits there and putrefies.

We have recommended breaths and techniques that massage the abdomen vigorously, ensuring that potentially dangerous clogging doesn't occur. For imaging, think of a river moving through you, flowing smoothly and inexorably around bends, coursing cleanly onward. Like a mighty river, the intestines never stop moving. We viewed the body of an imaging patient on a fluoroscope (an X-ray machine whose image registers on a television screen), and saw her intestines alive, moving gently, as if massaging themselves, while she had no sensation at all of the inner action.

Your body *is* alive. Even in gray moments of exhaustion and fatigue, it carries on a complex and incredible web of transformations. *Keep it alive.*

PELVIC IMAGING

Beneath the abdomen is the pelvis, where legs and spine come together. This nexus of large bones is the seat of basic body strength. A person not well adjusted there is ill-adjusted in general.

The key to pelvic imaging is the directing of images of space and freedom so that the legs feel loose enough to line up correctly. In that way, the lower body can move easily without unbalancing the upper body, and vice versa.

Breathing space and freedom and light and relaxation into the pelvic area benefits the muscles that align the spine and the pelvis and control the critical juncture. These are the psoas muscles. Physical action depends on the proper functioning of the psoas muscles. The psoas major ends at the hip, the psoas minor inserts into the pelvic girdle. Their tone is critical. If these muscles are weak or overly tight, legs, feet, and back may suffer. A registered physical therapist has told us that she finds that "a weakened psoas muscle is one of the primary causes of lower body pain and structural imbalance. I put much emphasis on strengthening the psoas through specific exercises and deep breathing." One particularly good image for breathing and for stretching is to "see" the psoas flexing and relaxing as needed, to keep legs and back straight and strong.

THE FEET

Here's how you can imagine your way into your feet:
Stand up and pull your shoulders back.
Imagine a clean line of energy flowing from your feet all the way to the top of your head.
Try to center your body over your feet.
Feel how the slightest adjustment in balance is reflected in a varying pressure on your feet.
As an essential part of the body, feet are your basic connection with the earth. Yet many people ignore their feet, never giving them a moment's thought. To enhance their sensitivity, spend some time barefoot each day. Your feet will thank you; after all, they spend so much time "on their feet," trapped inside shoes and boots.

BODY-TREE IMAGERY

Think of your body as a tree. Your feet are the roots, your legs the trunk, your chest and arms the spread of branches, your head the crown. Bend downward, in a squatting position for instance, then rise slowly while imagistically experiencing the natural upward evolution of a tree. Inhale fully and imagine fresh water flowing from the roots and out to every branch and leaf. This is a basic, revitalizing stretch.

Not long ago, a patient was suffering from edema, that is, from swelling in her legs. There didn't seem to be a cause for the condition. At our suggestion, she began practicing breathing techniques on a daily basis. She imagined inhaling lightness with each relaxing breath and exhaling heaviness, fluid, and tension through her legs and into the earth. After three days, she realized she had a powerful quantity of emotion bound up with her legs and that the emotion was related to a current family conflict. Because she had not been consciously in touch with this emotion, swelling and retention of fluid in her legs was its manifestation. Through the combination of breathing and imagery she became able to face the conflict. She recognized that she had to talk about it with the family member concerned. When she did, she removed the causative tension. Her breathing exercises came much easier in the days that followed. She inhaled lightness and breathed out tensions so effectively that in a few weeks the edema was cured. It had been simply a matter of getting in touch with her emotions and, through them, her body and its secrets.

PREGNANCY AND CHILDBIRTH

During pregnancy, various anxieties can arise for mother and father. It's perfectly natural. Unfortunately, blood flow can be affected when the mother is tense. Less nourishment goes to the fetus. Breathing for relaxation counteracts the tensions. Any relaxing abdominal breath is good. The Alternate Nostril Breath is especially good for clearing the mind, allowing physiology to return to calm normalcy.

Hypertension accompanies pregnancy, which is why breath can once again be a boon. A team of British researchers reported that relaxation exercises had a significant, positive effect on hypertension in pregnant women. It was welcome news, particularly because the results were achieved without drugs, most of which should be avoided during pregnancy.

Breathing in union with imagery can aid in the creation of emotional and psychological bonds between parents and fetus. Such bonds can be carried over into the postnatal phase of the child's life.

The time from conception to birth is a magical time. Two cells unite to form one that multiplies, transforms, and grows in the harmonious dance of new life. During the process, the basic elements of emotion and the areas of mental excellence and personality are formed. The fetus experiences emotional impressions, especially from the mother, but from other family members as well. It is of utmost importance to connect actively with the person being formed.

Bonding is nurturing to all involved. It brings out the true joy and wonder of the pregnancy phase of birth. Father and mother join to express love to the unborn child and to each other. A return to bonding helps to sustain the parents during the sometimes difficult experience of childrearing.

THE BONDING BREATH

The time from conception to birth is a magical time, as two cells unite to form one that multiplies, transforms, and grows in the harmonious dance of new life. During the process of the formation of a new body, the basic elements of the child's emotions, areas of mental excellence, and personality are beginning to form. These are modified during life after birth; however, it is important to note that the fetus does experience emotional impressions, especially from the mother, but from all other family members as well. It is of utmost importance to connect actively with the child. This bonding not only is nurturing to all involved but brings us back to the true joy and wonder of the pregnancy phase of life. The father and mother are joining together to express love to the unborn child and to each other. The bonding that occurs between the parents helps sustain them during the sometimes difficult experience of child-rearing. When the family experience becomes difficult, you can go back to that life-affirming time of bonding and re-experience deep love and emotions.

In the Bonding Breath, the pregnant woman lies comfortably on her back; her hands and her husband's rest on
her abdomen.
1. Perform the Abdominal Breath in unison, with eyes
   closed.
2. Visualize the baby in position for birth.
3. Visualize the baby's head dropping to engage in the
   pelvis.
4. Visualize the birth process proceeding smoothly.
5. Think of an affirmation, such as "We now feel the child
   and ourselves happy and strong."
6. Open your eyes slowly and relax for a few minutes,
   or longer if you want to. Feel the natural bond.

We suggest to parents that they invite children in the
family to join in the Bonding Breath, to feel part of the
birthing process.

Many childbirth methods incorporate breathing techniques before and during labor and delivery. As an illustra-
tion, we should like to share a thought on husband-coached
childbirth by Robert A. Bradley:

"Under your guidance she will learn to 'bulge' her
abdomen out actively, deliberately with each inspiration
and then let go and rhythmically let her abdomen drop
back down with expiration. The weight of your hand laid
lightly on her abdomen serves as a guide. She will feel the
rhythm of giving your hand a ride on the waves, up and
down, or a sensation that her abdomen is an accordion and
she is rhythmically opening and closing it to affect the
coming and going of air."

The pregnant woman should start to practice breathing
techniques long before labor is expected, and to do so in
non-stressful situations. If practiced, contractions of labor,
when they occur, will automatically trigger deep abdominal
breathing and the prospective mother will be able to
"breathe through" contractions. Breath significantly re-

duces labor pain. The woman "rolls with," rather than fights, the inevitable pain she has.

ASTHMA

Obviously, breathing techniques can be applied advanta-geously to the many kinds of respiratory trouble. Conditions such as asthma and respiratory allergies such as hay fever and sensitivity to animal hair can be alleviated. The Alternate Nostril Breath is especially good for this purpose.

According to the American Lung Association, asthma is the most common chronic childhood disease in the United States, affecting more than two million children and young teenagers at any given time. It is unrealistic to expect their asthma to vanish, but with proper management improve-ment can be expected, and many will be able to give up med-ication. Most hospitals and clinics have classes that people with breathing difficulties can attend. They teach breathing techniques and how to strengthen breathing capacity.

While the root cause of asthma remains unknown, an attack in those who are susceptible is usually triggered by stress to the bronchial tubes. This stress can be caused by cigarette smoke, smog, dust, strenuous exercise, or even shouting, whether in anger or, for instance, by joining in a standing cheer at a sports event. During an attack, bronchial tubes narrow due to constriction of their muscles, swelling of tissues, and secretion of mucus. It now takes a longer time to exhale through the narrowed tubes, and it is taxing. During inhalation, the diaphragm contracts; during exhalation, it merely relaxes, so there is less muscular assis-tance in breathing out; the rebound of compressed abdomi-nal organs doesn't make up for the difference.

Breathing exercises—nondrug therapy!—improve the full range of the asthmatic's respiration and expand the breathing apparatus. For optimal breathing and release of congestion, we recommend techniques like the Abdominal Breath and the Lung Expander and the Lung Strengthener:

THE LUNG STRENGTHENER

1. Do two to three minutes of the Abdominal Breath.
2. Perform five to ten minutes of the Alternate Nostril Breath.
3. Perform two to three minutes of Ujjai (the Whooshing Breath).
4. Imagine, during Ujjai, your lungs healthy and clear and your bronchial tubes relaxed. See clear, cleansing, and healing light bringing in health with each breath.
5. Affirm: "The stress in my lungs and chest will be released and my breathing will work optimally."
6. Finish with the Alternate Nostril Breath if you feel like it. Try to see to it that you are not interrupted during this technique. Perform the Alternate Nostril Breath for five to ten minutes.

The Lung Strengthener, which makes use of three breaths plus imagery, becomes easier with practice. The asthma sufferer who uses this technique must stay on his medication but may wish to consult with his physician about a possible reduction in amount.

There are many breathing therapy programs across the land, sponsored by lung associations and other groups. One fascinating school program has been Buddies for Better Breathing, in Tolland, Connecticut. A nurse, Irene Gay, and a physical educator, Fran Adamczyk, founded this program for asthmatic schoolchildren in 1979. Miss Gay told us that the project began as a self-help program that a child could use to try to avert an asthmatic episode.

The children in Tolland learn breath techniques like "forced expiration." They take a deep breath and exhale slowly through pursed lips. "Often," said Miss Gay, "controlled breathing alone can ward off an impending attack." They are taught to do situps to strengthen their stomach muscles so they "can use these muscles to force trapped air out of their lungs when beset with a serious attack." The boys and girls play many games to improve breathing ability. They blow a Ping-Pong ball across a table. They blow soap bubbles through hoops. They inflate balloons and paper bags, then pop them in a noisy contest.

There is a widely held impression that people with asthma should avoid heavy exercise and that children with asthma shouldn't compete at all in strenuous sports. We know several people with asthma who go regularly on long, strenuous backpacking trips and bear heavy loads. They tote their medication along, checking to be sure their self-medicating skills are up to par before they set out. Although exercise may bring on transient difficulty, they feel it is good for their asthmatic condition, because their lungs are strengthened.

Under certain circumstances, exercise can bring on respiratory symptoms in people who do not have asthma. In the chapter "The Sporting Life," we discuss the problem of adjusting lungs to winter's cold. In a woman who did not have asthma, we have observed an asthma-like wheeze directly after she had run in abnormally cold air. To some degree, everyone is sensitive to pulmonary stress.

If you have asthma and want to excel in sports, exercise caution and patience, consult your physician, but go for it. The sky's the limit. Keep in mind the example of the great mountaineer Hermann Buhl. He suffered from asthma but overcame his difficulties; his solo ascent of Nanga Parbat, an eight-thousand-meter peak in the western Himalayas, is a landmark in the history of alpinism.

(In a study by scientists at Yale University, vitamin C was found to reduce the intensity of asthma symptoms induced by exercise. Five hundred milligrams taken before a workout was an effective dose. Scientists in Nigeria found that vitamin C reduced the incidence of asthma attacks associated with the common cold and lessened the severity of those that occurred.)

SERIOUS RESPIRATORY DISTRESS

Until now, we have been talking about asthma sufferers who can, with a little effort, lead normal and active lives. What about those whose problems, whether from asthma or other respiratory disease, are intensely serious? Yes, even here breathing techniques, as an adjunct to medical attention, can be of significant help. M. K. Tandon, of the thoracic division of a hospital in Western Australia, uses breathing therapy for successful treatment of patients who have chronic severe airway obstruction. Treatment includes yoga postures and breathing exercises aimed at the maximal use of the entire abdominal and thoracic regions. Patients were matched with a control group that received standard physiotherapy only. Dr. Tandon found that "after training in yoga, the breathing pattern of the patients in the yoga group changed to a slower and deeper pattern, allowing them to tolerate higher work loads. On the other hand, the patients in the physiotherapy group did not change their shallow breathing patterns. The combination of breath technique with standard therapy proved to potentiate the beneficial effect."

ON ALCOHOL ABUSE

Breathing exercises alone will not cure alcoholism. But working with breath can be surprisingly effective in treating a different alcohol-related problem: reactive drinking.

Like compulsive refrigerator raiders, many drinkers automatically reach for the bottle when life gets rough—when they are passed over for promotion, when they have an argument with someone. This habit is destructive in terms both of health and of solving the problem that led to the reactive drink.

If pressure on the job leads to having an extra drink at lunch, the imbiber knows deep down that job performance will be hurt. Drinking makes many belligerent people even more volatile, more likely to say something they regret later. If things go badly and there is the temptation, the *need* to take a drink or two, use this tactic:

Take a few deep, relaxing Abdominal Breaths and generate some endorphin release and a calm, collected mood. The chances are good that a healthier, safer alternative will come to mind: talking out the frustration or exercising it off or having a glass of mineral water instead of a whiskey.

Social drinking can indeed be a problem. Parties, dinners, and business situations call for sharing a toast or downing a few while in the presence of others. If you wish to be courteous to those around you by joining in the celebration with a drink when you would prefer not to, introduce the philosophy we have been discussing throughout. Breathe naturally and focus on the benefits of the total body-mind harmony that is possible with an integrated self. Achieving the best and most satisfying experiences begins and ends psychologically with such harmony. Whether you want to unwind or to conclude a deal or just to maintain contacts in a drinking environment, breathe evenly and use the Relaxation Breath before having a drink. Establishing yourself is akin to grounding. You become serene, alert, unafraid, totally at peace. The deep resonance of the Relaxation Breath will bring a stability and a surety that hectic gulping can never match. You will not *need* to match others drink for drink. A side benefit of breathing techniques is that practice leads to creation of an atmosphere inside your strong self that discourages drinking to excess. Body and mind will be at ease without the artificial stimulus of drink.

These principles are especially important to remember at holiday times, when the pressure to lift a few extras can become tidal and all-consuming. Become even "higher" in your own eyes from satisfaction derived through deflecting excess.

Another kind of reactive drinking is initiated by a serious life trauma, such as the loss of a loved one or a broken relationship. The drinking may last until mourning is over, until the situation is resolved. Breathing techniques help. They are relaxing, they help to make contact with emotions. They allow the troubled to find the roots of distress more easily and avoid overindulgence in drink.

COMPULSIVE BEHAVIOR

Breathing can help to assuage other habits, such as nail-biting and hair-pulling. One young woman felt that she was close to becoming a suicide because of a highly resistant habit. Susan felt that things in her life had become meaningless. She had seen two psychiatrists and tried other therapies in trying to overcome the particular problem she was experiencing. She was eighteen years old and beautiful—and a hair-puller. She had had the habit for some four or five years before coming in for help. Despite the persistence of the habit, no one knew about it except her mother. Even her boyfriend didn't know. Because her hair was so severely mauled, she camouflaged her compulsion by wearing a wig. She had little of her own hair left by the time we first saw her.

When Susan disclosed her history, we learned that she had begun to pull her hair when forced to move with her family to a new city. Far away from friends, she found herself out of touch and alone, continually frightened at the growing sense that she was always going to be alone. She recalled retreating to a closet when she started to pull her hair. She wrapped her fingers in her hair and started to pull. And pull. And now, years later, she had come to the end of her rope. The idea that her boyfriend would learn that she wore a wig added to her distress.

We began treatment slowly, first teaching her to relax. Specific relaxation techniques were introduced so she would practice them instead of pulling her hair. We reasoned that the hair-pulling response was most likely to occur when she was nervous, lonely, bored, unable to relax. Whenever she had the pulling impulse, she was to concentrate instead on the diaphragmatic breathing we had taught her. It would induce the calmness she needed to overcome the recurring trauma.

The endorphins released in diaphragmatic breathing produced a sense of enjoyment, a high that augmented a sense of calm. Susan learned to deal successfully with her compulsion. While breathing thus, she visualized herself with beautiful, long, flowing locks. We asked her to establish a clear picture of what she wanted to look like, and to concentrate on that picture as she breathed. By combining imagery and breathing techniques, she was able to overcome her habit in a relatively brief time. She had learned to substitute positive life-giving techniques for the destructive hair-pulling that had been beyond her control. In time, her natural hair was restored fully and she pitched her wig into a trash barrel.

HYPERVENTILATION AND PANIC

Breathing techniques help alleviate many symptoms of psychological distress. Hyperventilation is a prime symptom of panic or high anxiety. Sometimes, physical exertion in intense heat will bring on hyperventilation.

Basically, stress causes a nervous acceleration of respiration. Breath accelerates until the victim is panting at a tremendous rate. There is now a fascinating occurrence: because lungs can get rid of carbon dioxide quicker than they can absorb oxygen, super-quick, shallow, panicked breaths cause the carbon dioxide level in the blood to drop. Oxygenation slows. The body's automatic, unconscious regulation of breathing takes its major cue from the level of carbon dioxide in the blood. If the carbon dioxide level rises, the lungs are signaled to breathe deeper. When carbon dioxide goes down in hyperventilation, the regular mechanism tells the lungs not to breathe as much. The paradoxical state in which one consciously pants as fast as possible is eventually attained and the unconscious, automatic regulatory shuts down deep breathing in the lungs. The victim's face becomes redder and redder, he makes a terrific amount of noise, he is barely taking in enough oxygen to remain conscious. This painful condition, called dyspnea, is often part of an acute anxiety attack. Aside from the inability to breathe, the victim may feel nausea, palpitations, dizziness, chest pain, and a sense that his imminent demise is at hand.

There is good news for those who suffer from anxiety attack, phobic reaction, and attendant hyperventilation. Many researchers discovered that training in diaphragmatic breathing could be used as an effective tool in reducing or eliminating panic reactions and hyperventilation. For a British study, patients suffering from agoraphobia (fear of open places) were taught to breathe deeply with their diaphragms. After a six-month follow-up, they were found to be doing significantly better than the control group, which had received only standard therapy. The practiced ability to breathe deeply at will enabled the experimentees to break the cycle of hyperventilation and to avoid the worst symptoms of their fears. Abdominal breathing turns out to be also a handy and valuable tactic for anyone who finds himself in a frightening situation.

SINUS CONGESTION

Even the best unpolluted, invigorating ocean air will do you little good if your sinuses are stuffed, thereby preventing free breathing. Sinus congestion dulls the sense of taste.

Life in general becomes less fun. Millions of people suffer from sinusitis or repeated stuffiness from colds. Symptoms may linger after the cold is otherwise gone. Fortunately, breathing techniques have been found effective in freeing clogged sinuses. The Kapalabhati, Ha!, and Alternate Nostril breaths are especially helpful. It is merely a matter of finding the specific technique that works best.

We have discussed rubbing the occipital points in the back of the head to relieve stuffiness, and we have recommended putting pressure under the armpit opposite the blocked or stuffed nostril. Here is another technique worth trying:

Just before doing Kapalabhati, do sinus-tapping. Use the index and the middle fingers of one hand to tap quickly both sides of the nose just below the eyes and just above the bridge of the nose and the forehead. This should help to free the mucus that is clinging to the sinuses; forceful Kapalabhati exhalations will drain it out. (Keep tissues handy.)

If you are suffering from sinusitis or a head cold, and the "poisons" have not been eliminated, you should avoid certain foods such as sugar, white flour, and salt, as well as dairy foods, fried foods, and fatty meats, if you haven't already been doing so. For most people, these foods encourage the formation of excessive mucus, keeping sinuses stuffed. This in turn leads to breathing through the mouth and the entry of more pollutants. This additional "garbage" makes it even more troublesome to breathe, further disrupting the body's delicate chemical balancing act.

For the common condition of sinusitis, we recommend the use of vaporizers, tea kettles, or plasters. Vaporizers, particularly those using an herbal emulsion, help to thin the obstructive mucus so that the respiratory tree can release it. Thick, tenacious mucus is hard to free up, but the vaporizer will help.

An herbal preparation to use in the vaporizer is eucalyptus oil. (It is used in saunas.) It is available in most pharmacies. The addition of four or five drops of the oil to vaporizer water or to a pan of boiling water makes for superior penetration of the vapor and aromatic air. Drinking lots of fluids, especially natural fruit juice and water, also acts to thin the mucus.

Another helpful treatment is the use of ginger. It helps to break up excess mucus and reduce inflammation that caused the excess congestion initially. Chop up two teaspoonfuls of fresh ginger and put them into two cups of water. Boil for twenty minutes. Use as a steam with eucalyptus or drink plain as a tea.

Another treatment: Put a half teaspoon of red pepper (cayenne) into a glass of orange juice or tomato juice and drink it down quickly. In thirty seconds, the whole head and upper body area feel afire. Sweating breaks out. Better be near a sink, for there is the possibility that tremendous amounts of mucus will come flooding out.

The "jalapeño effect" has not escaped the notice of the medical community. Dr. Irwin Ziment, a lung specialist at the Los Angeles County–Olive View Medical Center, reported that he "encourages our respiratory patients who are having trouble with a build-up of mucus to eat spicy foods, as well as to take a lot of fluids, just as part of their daily regimen. We're not putting forth anything particularly original here. In a famous English medical text written three hundred and fifty years ago, the use of garlic to combat congestion is mentioned. This is an old folk remedy that is common in many countries."

Hot food is not for everyone. It can upset digestion and aggravate hemorrhoids. Hot pepper doesn't blend well with all kinds of cuisine. But if you like burning your insides out, go ahead and clear those sinuses!

ALLERGIES

Many of us experience some kind of respiratory allergy to mold or pollen or animal hairs. Techniques such as Kapalabhati and the Alternate Nostril Breath help to keep air passages open during a severe allergic attack. The steams and teas mentioned previously can do wonders to keep the nasal cavity open. The next time your least favorite allergy comes around, give the natural form of treatment a try. It's nothing to sneeze at.

SLEEP

Sleep is deeply connected with breathing and overall respiratory health. The Federal government's Project Sleep discovered that the sleep of almost 50 million Americans is troubled by insomnia!

It was once thought that not much could be done to help those who slept poorly. But there is now good news here as well. Researchers at Stanford University discovered that the ability to sleep well can be *learned*. Among the tools employed in a pilot program for insomniac patients were, as might be expected, relaxation exercises. And what better relaxation exercise than slow, deep breathing!

For people with sleeping disorders or disturbances, a good way to create the necessary emotional climate is to slow down breathing and reverse the "arousal mechanism."

In bed, start by focusing all thoughts on the process of breathing in and out. While thus focused, it is impossible for you simultaneously to think about the problems and vexations causing insomnia. Repeated breathing in and breathing out has the same lulling, calming effect as a mantra or as counting sheep. In a sense, it is better than either; oxygen replenishes and rebuilds—double dipping.

The basis of the technique is abdominal breathing. But this relaxing breath will not work optimally if it's not done during the day as well. Do it during the course of the day, and then again at night.

Dr. Migdow suggests the following pattern for his patients who have trouble sleeping:

1. *Waking:* Take four or five minutes to (a) stretch all of your muscles like a cat; (b) yawn and sigh; (c) rub areas that are stiff.

2. *After getting ready for the day's work:* (a) Take slow, deep breaths for five minutes; inhale into the abdomen and squeeze it on the exhalation; (b) imagine tension leaving your body; experience your mind letting go of fears and anxieties; (c) bend and stretch any parts (such as neck, back, toes) that may be especially tense; (d) *affirm* that you have the strength and the flexibility to deal with any troubling occurrences that may come up during the day.

3. *Going to work:* (a) Listen to soothing music on your Walkman or in your car or sing or hum to yourself; (b) avoid tension-creating music or talk shows; (c) avoid letting your mind slip into tension or fear; (d) stretch your arms, legs, and neck when you are able; (e) keep your spirits up and loose.

4. *During the workday:* (a) Take two to three minutes each hour to stop what you are doing and duplicate the breathing process of Number 2 above; (b) stretch any part of your body that is tense; allow yourself to sigh to release tension; (c) bend your neck in all directions; roll your shoulders and back to get any kinks out. Return to your task clear and refreshed.

5. *During the day, if emotional tension arises:* (a) Take a deep breath into the abdomen; (b) release the breath fully and relax muscles during exhalation—especially neck, shoulders, back; (c) smile externally and internally to relax the face and to shift mood; (d) deal with any conflict in a more open, free state—have fun with it.

6. *At lunch:* Take ten to fifteen minutes to exercise. Walk or swim or jog or do yoga stretching to boost circulation.

Get outdoors; fresh air and sunshine are important.

7. *After the day is over:* Do two to three minutes as in Number 4 above.

8. *Returning home:* Affirm and feel the productivity of the day, as in Number 3 above.

9. *Shifting into home duties:* Make your transitions slowly, so that tension doesn't crop up.

10. *Prior to sleep:* This fairly simple bedtime breath may nevertheless prove somewhat difficult if the mind is full of thoughts and the body filled with tension.
(A) Do the Stress-Discharging technique first to release bodily tension; (b) do some Ujjai Breathing to release mental tension; (c) now, feeling more calm and peaceful, embark on slow silent breathing, inhaling four counts, exhaling eight counts. Remember to be as comfortable as possible. That comfort includes releasing stress built up during the day. Keep a pad and pencil near your bed so that you can write down good ideas as they pop into your head. Go into...Sweet Dreams.

If you are a normal sleeper, you can drift off breathing to a rhythm: four in, eight out, for example, as you lie on your back, the most efficient position for breathing. Use imagery to visualize your breath moving in and out. Imagine a soft, nurturing breeze moving in, moving out, spreading softly, covering your body from head to toes. As you become sleepy, shift to a more comfortable position and continue breathing to the rhythm.

SNORING

Snoring may seem to be merely an amusing annoyance. But aside from its disruptive effect on relationships, it is evidence of blocked nasal passages that should be attended to.

Many snorers are thoracic-breathers and mouth-breathers. They could benefit—as could any sleeper—by striving to keep the sinuses clear. Clear sinuses naturally make it easier to breathe through the nose. By practicing nose-breathing and the Abdominal Breath ten to twenty minutes a day, unconscious breathing can be gradually developed. Breathing deeply, regularly, and diaphragmatically through the nose will become second nature.

Snoring can result in sleep apnea, a condition in which the soft tissues of the throat that rattle to make a snoring noise can become so relaxed so flaccid, as to close the airway entirely. Multiple hiatuses in breathing can last ten seconds or more. Resulting high blood pressure and lack of oxygen are a predisposing factor that contributes to heart disease, especially in men.

GETTING UP IN THE MORNING

Getting to sleep effectively is only part—albeit a major part—of the bed battle. There is also the psychologically important moment of awakening in the morning.

Many people start their days in a grumpy mood. They are drowsy, feel lousy, snap testily. They just can't get their motors started. The Ha! Breath is particularly useful in waking up in the morning. (It also energizes the body through the day.)

A little complicated compared with the Ha!, but excellent for setting the tone for the day ahead, is the Rise-and-Shine Breath. You are lying on your back in bed when you begin:

THE RISE-AND-SHINE BREATH

1. Inhale through your nose and raise your arms perpendicular to the bed.
2. Exhale through your mouth while letting your arms drop.
3. Repeat Steps 1 and 2 slowly six times.
4. Inhale deeply and hold your breath for ten to fifteen seconds, or a bit longer if comfortable.
5. Exhale forcefully while pulling your stomach in, then sit up.

6. Inhale and reach for the sky while sitting.
7. Exhale, pulling your hands down to your shoulders and making fists.
8. Repeat Steps 6 and 7 five times.
9. Get out of bed. You're ready for the day.

PHYSICAL LIMITATIONS

For those with physical limitations, the emotional stress of their social singularity can be as much a burden as their physical impairment, particularly in America, the land of images. In Europe, visible imperfections in individuals are much more easily tolerated, perhaps because so many wars with wounds so visible have been contested there. In the United States, people unable to see, hear, or speak, or who have lost the use of limbs (about 32 million Americans are handicapped) experience enormous stress; the United States is not geared to the handicapped. (Even book publishers shy away from books designed to aid and comfort the handicapped; *Sexual Tips for the Physically Handicapped* is a proposal still in search of a publisher.)

People with physical limitations can use basic Relaxation Breaths to help let off excess stress, to unburden themselves of anger and repressed emotions. The techniques are practical and useful, and can be practiced by almost any impaired individual. Relaxation Breaths help one deal with the routines of daily life. Using the techniques for vitality helps to raise what is often a lagging level of bodily energy, and facilitates the reaching of maximum potential.

The same techniques work well with those who are temporarily impaired. The process of recovery can be doubly debilitating in such cases, because one is unaccustomed to being laid up or immobilized and faced with new fears and emotions; life-style has to be altered, at least temporarily. A good deal of pain may be integral to the problem. While dealing with it, one must face some unsettling questions:

Will recovery be complete? How long will recovery take? Will I be able to perform at the same level of play as before? Favored techniques should take over.

DENTAL WORK

Another painful situation can be that fidgety moment when one finds oneself once again in the "hot seat" of the dentist's chair. The mouth seems to wince in advance, the probings and assaults ripe in imagination. Tension reigns, blood pressure goes up. A mild but palpable state of panic takes over. The relaxing Abdominal Breath can come to the rescue again. Immediately. Right then and there. In the chair. If the hygienist looks quizzical, explain when the Breath is finished. Doing the Abdominal Breath allows one to be cooperative and at ease in the distinctly unnatural situation of the invasion of the mouth by a pair of plastic-coated hands, various metal probes, and sundry devices. It is an unenviable situation. But with the right breathing and the right attitude, the patient can find himself at least minimally accommodating. Roll with it. Anticipate the movements of the head needed to help the dentist reach the appropriate tooth surfaces.

Yes, hard as it is to believe, breath control can make a visit to the dentist's office bearable for the most timid soul. Serious breathers even disdain novocaine when having their teeth drilled. It's not all *that* bad, as we can testify from personal experience, once the rhythm of deep, slow breathing is under way.

You may not want to try something so "advanced" right off, but at the very least you'll be more relaxed and will endure less residual pain. Because the tension of expectation will have been lowered through relaxation, there will be a significant reduction in the after-office aching that one often experiences.

DOCTOR VISITS

The same relaxing techniques can be employed, of course, when visiting a medical doctor. Visitors to the doctor's office tend to worry, on some level, about blood-drawing, exploratory probing, painful injections, and the post-examination discussion of findings. Anticipatory fear is usually the worst part of the visit. Worry is not productive. Shuck it. Worry cannot solve, answer, cure, or help anything.

True, the doctor does occasionally have something "diabolical" up his sleeve. Occasionally, he must perform some unpleasant test—unpleasant for you. But for the most part, the discomfort is soon over. Breathing aimed, as it were, at the specific infusion of energy into a damaged part of the body may be undertaken. Imaging plays an important role here. As you sit in the anteroom, be quiet, relax, say goodbye to the worrying part of yourself, begin to do slow, deep breaths, then image the part of you that is imperfect or hurt and for whose rehabilitation you have come to the medical professionals.

SHIELDING

The Shielding Breath is detailed in the chapter on stress. It is especially helpful when you are feeling physically ill and emotionally vulnerable. There is a variation on this Breath. After Relaxation Breathing, imagine yourself breathing into a solid light. When you exhale, that light expands into a bubble around your whole being. Imagine yourself enveloped in the bubble—it is like an impervious space suit or a geodesic dome. Feel yourself being watched over, protected, safeguarded.

An important concept of the holistic approach to medicine underlying our successful techniques is that the body, mind, emotions, and spirit coexist—they all live in a mixing, fusing state of being, ultimately inseparable. Any time there is mental or emotional imbalance, that imbalance will also show itself somewhere in the body. Damage will occur in a state of subtle interaction with interrupted or impaired emotional and mental functioning. It is for this reason that the techniques discussed really work.

SEX

Heavy breathing. Right! Absolutely! Sex play is exercise, and exercise is the marriage of breath to movement. Breath can be used effectively to build sexual energy.

During sexual activity, breathing patterns change from a normal, quiet, resting pattern to nearly full capacity. In most cases it is fulfilling when the change is gradual and the breathing is deep, like an orchestra building to a crescendo. This biological breathing is more likely to occur if one is relaxed when activity begins.

Slow, deep breathing lets the body decide on its own rhythm. The wisdom of the body dominates uncertainties and anxieties of mind.

Breathing for relaxation overcomes both impotence in men and failure to reach orgasm in women—*and* that widespread bugaboo, performance anxiety. Much performance anxiety derives from the idea that in sexual activity ego is on the line. The mistake of viewing sexiness and potency as "trendy" and "status" is often made—trying to live up to an image rather than being oneself. Better to be free of the compulsion of "having to have sex." Compulsive behavior isn't much fun; neither is it a true expression of love. Breathing for relaxation prior to lovemaking allows mind and body to join in harmony and express true love through the channels of the body.

A humorous note: An annoying, but not serious, health problem is called "honeymoon nose." Briefly, this is a stuffy nose associated with the enthusiastic sexual activity common during some honeymoons. Beneath the mucous membrane inside the nose is erectile tissue, like that of the genital organs. This tissue may become engorged with blood in a sympathetic reaction to zealous sexual performance. We are not sure why, but an overload of sexual input may spill over to the nasal tissue, causing the swelling. Heavy breathing slows, as does sexual activity. Maybe it is the body's way of telling the couple to slow down and go about other business for a while.

If sex stimulates the nose, can deep breathing through the nose stimulate the sex organs? The mysteries of life are never-ending.

ENERGY

This is the basis of all we've discussed in this chapter. Again, health is not just a thorough yearly examination. It is the *feeling* of vibrancy and calm on all levels of being. Health is the state of a steady, balanced energy flow. When one feels this flow, one feels healthy, one has energy. When one doesn't, one feels ill or down or sick. Through the use of our constant companion, Breath, and with a little help from the power of imagination, one can create higher levels of health for oneself, thus reaching life's full potential.

CHAPTER EIGHT

MORE CASE HISTORIES

That is where [Sidd Finch] said he had learned to pitch...up in the mountains, flinging rocks [and breathing] and meditating.
          —George Plimpton, in *Sports Illustrated*

By now you, too, should be admiring the flexibility, practicality, and absolute ease with which conscious breathing can be incorporated into your life and how it improves the overall quality, clarity, and vigor of each and every day. You have learned how to direct your own breath toward aches you want to release and toward areas you would like to enhance.

Directing the potency of your breath is like uncovering a kind of Fort Knox of currency you never knew you had. Like money, breath can be spent wisely, with shrewd application and investment and glorious returns. Or it can be spent unwisely, erratically, without intelligence, bankrupting your personality. The choice is always yours.

There are millions of professional athletes, businesspeople, artists, and doctors—and writers, editors, and typists—

who recognize that breath is a key to the overall refinement (even in the evolutionary sense) of the system called body. The practice of controlled breathing is nothing but a further step toward evolutionary optimal efficiency and fullness of life.

By now, you should be feeling energized in a calm, stable way. Feel like moving a little? Let's move into the Stepping-Out Breath. Almost all of us walk, and walking can become an activity to gain optimal health and well-being. Here we use the breath and movement in harmonious fashion to create a lightness in movement and feeling and a straightness and strength to our structure. This combination of lightness and strength allows us to be firm, yet flexible. It helps us keep a light, happy outlook, which we all would like to experience more often.

THE STEPPING-OUT BREATH

1. Inhale for four steps while walking and expanding your chest.
2. Exhale for eight steps, pulling in your stomach.
3. Allow your back to straighten. Stand tall and proud as you inhale.
4. Imagine, as you exhale, that you feel the tension flowing out of your neck and back.
5. Feel the strength in your step and the rhythm in your arms.
6. Inhale deeply at the end of the walk and let out a sigh, releasing chest tension. You may wish to inhale and sigh several times.

You feel terrific, don't you?

And if you really want to fly, head right into...

THE HIGH-PERFORMANCE BREATH

1. Take a few Abdominal Breaths while standing.
2. Snap your right leg up and back in one motion as you take a Ha! Breath, hitting the heel of your foot against

your right buttock, then letting the foot drop to the floor.

3. Snap your left leg up and back in one motion, as you take a Ha! Breath, hitting the heel against the left buttock, then letting the foot drop to the floor.

4. Repeat Steps 2 and 3 ten to fifteen times.

5. Extend your arms in front of you and make fists with your hands.

6. Pull back the right fist quickly to your chest with the Ha! Breath.

7. Repeat with the left fist.

8. Do alternate pulling, right-left, ten to thirty times, as though you were pulling in a rope.

9. Squat, inhale, hold your breath, then exhale with a Ha! as you leap up with your arms extended.

The key to experiencing life more fully is energy. We search for energy externally, but never seem totally fulfilled.

When we begin to look within ourselves, we find all the energy we need, moment to moment.

Breath is the key to unlocking our inner energy and vitality.

Say you've been reading this book, either alone or aloud with a friend, and you experience an insight into yourself, your health, and your energy. Celebrate this new insight with...

THE BREATH OF JOY

1. Stand with your arms at your sides, relaxed and in good posture. On a slow, steady inhalation, raise your arms horizontally until they are even with your shoulders; then move your arms in front of you; finally, raise your arms over your head.

2. Hold your breath for a moment.

3. Exhale through your mouth and make the Ha! sound while dropping your head, neck, shoulders, and arms.

4. Repeat Steps 1, 2, and 3 three to five times. You'll notice your joy as you loosen into the exhalation. You will smile spontaneously and often.

By becoming aware of your internal and external movements, you permit yourself the experience of both a deep richness of life and the continuous, life-affirming flow of energy. Once you are aware of yourself, you can consciously use the energies to experience greater health, peace, and fulfillment, and move toward and through inner transformation.

Use of breath can lead to a change in diet. The foods you hungered for begin to lose their appeal. You begin to realize that the appeal was simply more than the force of hunger. You try whole foods for a change. You notice the marked difference. You notice that through directed breathing while chewing and eating, whole foods last longer and taste better than refined foods. You begin to relish whole foods, with their richness, texture, and taste. Presently, you are indeed healthier.

You begin to question more. One Sunday afternoon, during the football season, while glued to your television box and beer and chips, you will decide you would rather be *playing*. You have the energy to do it. Breathing will lift you out of the realm of the armchair enthusiast.

Through breathing, you become more efficient, you have more time, you indeed have more energy. Old habits that translated into poor health—habits like overeating, over-drinking coffee and alcohol, smoking—are now less desirable. Naturally, without the strain of previous attempts, you will begin to moderate these things.

We cannot repeat enough the obvious benefits of relaxed, conscious breathing. Consider it this way:

You have three meals a day. You need food for nutrients. You breathe an average of fifteen times every minute, at least twenty thousand times a day, awake, asleep, thinking, exercising, working, loafing. You never stop breathing. Think of all the energy you put into breathing.

Through breathing, you get more into the experience of complete living. This can happen through the most mundane of experiences. By challenging the present order of things, experiences can become more uplifting. More and more, the moment of continual exuberance can be created in everything you do.

"I CALM DOWN RIGHT AWAY."

Bill Nuessle, a clinical psychologist, in Lenox, Massachusetts, has been breathing consciously, working with breath patterns and techniques, for over 20 years. This is his success story in a capsule:

"I have been working with breath control in different ways: yogic breathing exercises, running, exercises for the effect they had on my breathing, and meditation. The Ujjai Breath has been the most effective of the yogic breathing exercises, and it is the technique I use most. Ujjai is pharyngeal breathing—you inhale using the muscles at the back of your throat rather than the muscles of your nostrils. A soothing, deep, whooshing sound is part of Ujjai. When I am under stress or feel emotionally upset, I trigger in this breath and calm down right away. It is like having a nonaddictive tranquilizer on call."

"MY INSTRUMENT BECOMES A PART OF ME."

Alfred V. Brown, a professional musician, began playing the violin at the age of seven:

"I switched to the viola when I was about fifteen. At about the same time, a teacher impressed upon me the significance of breath to playing. Wind and brass players learn the importance of breath when they first take up their instruments; it is an integral part of their technique. For a string player the concept of breathing is not so obvious. The bow represents the breath for a violinist: it produces the vibrating string (the equivalent of the air column in a wind instrument) upon which the notes are played. Because phrasing (putting groups of musical notes together) is accomplished with the bow, it is essential that the performer breathe with the phrase. If this is done correctly, emotions and feelings can be channeled harmoniously through the instrument. Many musicians grunt, groan, hum, or even sing while playing. Casals, Rubinstein, and Gould vocalized their breathing to a certain degree. While playing a phrase, I, for one, try to imagine how a fine vocalist would sing it, and I breathe the way the singer would. If I can do this successfully, my instrument becomes a part of me rather than a thing apart."

"IT IS JUST ABOUT IMPOSSIBLE TO FEEL STRESSED."

Whether you operate a subway train or a jet plane, teach the first grade, or are a forest ranger, you are a specialist and you respond to demands and stresses and responsibilities in your own individual way. Ronald Dushkin, M.D., who practices holistic medicine in New York City, teaches business managers how to manage their breathing. He calls his classes "stress management and wellness" seminars. Conscious breathing and the various ways it is applied have played an important part in both his personal and professional days.

"I find that deep Abdominal Breathing is helpful in a number of ways. It is an effective, a very effective, stress-management technique. It is just about impossible to feel stressed while doing Abdominal Breathing correctly.

"I use the breath to help me make transitions in day-to-day life. I will take one deep breath before seeing a patient and one as he or she goes out the door. The combination helps me move smoothly into my next activity, whether it is seeing another patient, taking a phone call, or attending a meeting.

"It didn't take me long to realize that my approach to the way I deal with my activities would be taught to others, even though their lives are usually completely different from my own. Abdominal Breath is one of the most significant skills I offer at seminars. It is by far the best right-now, on-the-spot relaxation skill. As I tell people, 'You need to keep breathing, and all of us can breathe to advantage.' Directed breathing helps us to focus on what's happening in the moment, not before or later.

"I advise businessmen and businesswomen to begin and end meetings with one or two deep breaths. Some have written later to say that the breaths led to creative problem-solving. If a businessperson, or anyone for that matter, takes the time to sit quietly and breathe abdominally, fully inhaling and exhaling at a certain rhythm for three to five minutes, he or she can move into any situation with an overflow of mental clarity.

"In my medical office, I recommend deep breathing to all my patients. If someone is going through a stressful time, I write a prescription to 'take two deep breaths before meals and at bedtime, and as needed.' The simple act of stopping to take two deep breaths slows you down. The breaths become an automatic relaxation technique.

"I introduce a few simple techniques when teaching basic anatomy and physiology to groups (e.g., yoga teachers, people with respiratory problems, smokers). Having someone blow up a balloon illustrates vividly what lungs look like during inhalation. The size of the balloon is dependent on the amount of air blown into it. If the blower breathes shallowly, only a small part of the balloon fills. It is a signal to proceed to the Lung Expander technique.

"I have another demonstration that illustrates lung volume. Fill a clear one-gallon plastic container with colored water. If you breathe shallowly, you use only a little bit more than a pint of air for each breath. To demonstrate this fact, pour one pint of colored water into an empty pint-size container (the inhalation) and pour it out to demonstrate the exhalation. Your capacity to take a full breath is nearly seven times that amount—almost four quarts. If you pour the whole gallon of liquid into an empty gallon-size container, you will never want to breathe shallowly again. You will want to breathe big with every breath you draw.

"I also have a graphic demonstration to stimulate smokers to quit. Take a gallon of liquid that had herb or tea leaves sprinkled in it. Place a clean sponge in the liquid and let it soak up some water, then squeeze it out. You will see that the sponge is clotted with leaves. *That* is what lungs look like after deep-breathing cigarette smoke."

HE LEARNED TO TAKE COMMAND.

A man in Denver had two major coronaries. Three quarters of his heart was damaged in the second attack and his life was in danger. That was a decade ago. Today, he operates a number of businesses and leads an active life. He is convinced that the thing that helps him to deal successfully with his health problems is careful management of stress. Doctors warned him that stress would be his downfall; he must avoid sudden bursts of adrenaline, because his heart would be too weak to handle the strain. He had to control emotions, attitudes, and stresses; he had to maintain a good sense of balance at all times to avoid setting off his biological alarm. He learned to take command of his life by using diaphragmatic breathing techniques that stabilize his metabolism.

"RELAXATION CARRIES OVER INTO ALL ACTIVITIES."

Unfortunately, many contemporary jobs, like data processing, have built-in tension-producing features that become magnified over time. Desk-sitting, bus-driving, and computer-terminal-staring—our systems are crippled by day's end. Fortunately, all over America people are catching on. They are learning that through conscious breathing they can be liberated from the strains that tend to become the norm. Cynthia Casterella, who lives in western Massachusetts, initiated change in her own life, and she is now a stress-management consultant helping others. She says:

"Teaching people how to adapt to stress paves the way to understanding the transformation of that very stress into positive energy for living more fully and happily. The techniques I teach involve psychophysical exercises that relax tensions in muscles and organs, relaxation skills to center the mind, and behavioral skills, such as time management, attitudinal awareness, communication, and problem-solving. Breathing techniques are incorporated as powerful aids to calming the autonomic nervous system.

"This is how I bring a class to order: I say, 'Sit erect, yet relaxed, and close your eyes. Let your facial muscles relax, especially your forehead, eyes, and jaw. Take a few deep, even breaths through your nose, allowing the relaxation you start to feel spread throughout your whole body...your face...your neck and shoulders...your arms and hands ...your torso, especially your abdomen...feeling it flowing into your hips, legs, and feet. With each breath, feel the warm energy radiating into your body. With each exhalation, experience the letting-go of tension and tightness. Relax your abdomen. Allow it to rise and fall with breath. Inhaling, the abdomen expands; exhaling, it falls back in. Observe this easy motion of breath...in and out, rising and falling. Gradually allow the breath to find its own rhythm...don't manipulate it, just watch it...allow the breath to "breathe you"...let any thoughts float by...gradually return your attention to the breath...in and out, rising and falling...be fully with each moment, with the simple, natural cycle.'

"Usually, two to five minutes of this is sufficient to center a class. (It is a technique that is wonderful to perform in the peace and quiet of your home, especially after tucking the kids in for the night.) I try to set a noncompetitive atmosphere. I teach the men and women, the boys and girls, to work with and to come to understand their personal limits and needs.

"When we do yoga postures or slow movement exercises, breathing is synchronized with each movement. If arms are stretched upward, the movement is done as though calibrated with an inhalation. Just as the fullest stretch is attained, the fullest lung capacity is reached as well. Exhalation is calibrated to downward motion, ending as the arms return to the starting position. As students learn this coordination of breath and movement, postures of exercise become 'meditations in motion.' Overall relaxation carries over into all activities and imparts new energy and gracefulness."

"BREATHING *IS* ENERGY."

A singer who is also a body therapist told us:

"Singing is a sport. It is a sport in the sense that it depends on concentrated direct energy to be effective. It requires a warm-up period before the performance in order to be successful and fulfilling. Singing is the first *hara* exercise that most of us participate in as youngsters. Crying and shrieking are forms of *hara*. We learn to interact with the people around us by manipulating our voices and later—with refinement—manipulating certain responses by varying our sounds. We learn to direct where those sounds originate.

"Through experience and training, I have discovered that my singing teachers were right all along. The power that makes a singer worth listening to is all about energy, all about breathing into and out of the abdomen, the *hara*. My experiences in sports (swimming, running, weightlifting, bicycling, scuba diving) are also directed through the breath. They *all* call for conscious use of the power I have and the length of time I have to work on the problem and where I wish to accentuate more or less power. I compare this to making a peanut butter sandwich. A true lover of peanut butter knows exactly how to spread it so the slice of bread is covered carefully and evenly and there's no peanut butter hanging over the edge of the bread and there's no mush when a second slice is placed on top. So it is with breath in singing and sports.

"In order to warm up for sports, everyone knows he must first stretch his muscles to prevent tears and other injuries. Every singer needs to warm up, too. I have found that certain exercises are particularly effective.

"Here's what I do to get into the flow, to 'hook up.' I stand up straight. I inhale completely. With a powerful exhalation I thrust arms and elbows behind me. I do this repeatedly, exhaling with a Ha! I assume a squatting position to energize my entire body. I inhale in the squat position, curling my head in. I use breath to exhale: Ha! I move into a standing position. I do this ten times.

"A terrific way to warm up is to do it outdoors. You absorb energy offered by nature.

"During my career as a vocalist I have been amused by the number of people who come up to me and marvel at my ability to sing. (Or so they say.) Almost all of them were actually responding to my *energy*. They believed I was doing something they could not do. It is true that many of the most popular singers around do not have exceptional voices. They *do* have a fantastic sense of how to direct their energy. I mean that literally. *They know how to breathe. Breathing is* energy."

"...REOXYGENATES MY BLOOD."

We received a letter from a woman who had returned to her apartment in New York City from a visit to India. She made herself begin a regular routine of yoga postures, breathing exercises, and meditation:

"Having experienced firsthand the correlation between breath and mind, I have experimented with the Kapalabhati and Alternate Nostril Breath. When I need extra energy, I do Kapalabhati to reoxygenate my blood. I quickly move from any draggy feeling to one of high spirits and positive energy. When I feel nervous, irritable, or unbalanced, I use the Alternate Nostril Breath that will also calm my mind. I find that if I am having trouble sleeping, abdominal breathing with breath-holding will usually lead me into dreamland. I have learned to jog a few miles, sprinting at the end so that I am drawing in lungfuls of fresh air. Controlled breathing is wonderful."

AFTER TWO MONTHS, HE FELT JOY.

He was thirty-seven years old and tired all the time. He couldn't get himself out of bed in the morning and he was having trouble on the job. He had had mononucleosis and hepatitis, but even after a complete recovery he was still chronically fatigued. An enlightened doctor recommended the slow, rhythmic Relaxation Breath. Twice a day for ten minutes, on the job or at home, he practiced the Relaxation Breath while imagining himself becoming energized. He began to feel better and better with every passing day. After two months, he felt joy—sheer, unencumbered joy—for the first time in years. As a sign to himself that he was "cured," he took up flying his private plane again.

"HAVING A STREAM TO TAKE A COOL DIP IN."

She was twenty-nine years old and had been a teacher since graduation from college. With each year, she disliked going into the classroom more and more. She piled up stress upon stress as she did the same monotonous things over and over and over. She had gone into teaching because she believed herself to have a natural talent with children. They had been drawn to her and she to them. But even while teaching the school's best children she was now abrupt, irritable, snappish. In desperation, she consulted a fellow teacher. Should she be taking tranquilizers? Should she see a psychiatrist? The friend suggested she try the Relaxation Breath for five minutes every day. She had nothing to lose; what are five minutes? She began doing the Relaxation Breath before eating her lunch. She began practicing the Ha! Breath each evening. She realized she was becoming refreshed, even energized. She likened her breathing techniques to "having a stream to take a cool dip in." She is married now, joyously raising a daughter, and is back at teaching, never happier.

"I PERSEVERED AND THINGS BECAME EASIER, BETTER."

A woman in Canada told us about the positive power of breath control:

"In early 1966, I was diagnosed as having bronchiectasis on both lungs, the condition being slightly worse on the left side. I took the doctor's advice and underwent a partial lower left lobectomy. (Removal of even part of a lung is not an experience I would wish on anyone.) Various doctors fed me antibiotics to control the infections. But the net effect was that the infections increased in frequency until I was having attacks of bronchiectasis (or pneumonia) six times a winter.

"For twelve years I had moderate to severe chest pain as well as frequent attacks of bronchiectasis, bronchitis, severe colds, flu, and sinusitis. Five doctors whom I told of chest pain informed me I wasn't having chest pain. I chose not to mention chest pain to the new doctor, who sent me to a hospital for breathing tests. He at once saw that my performances, which included inhalation tests, showed evidence of a great deal of tightness or constriction in the bronchial tubes. 'You must have been in a lot of pain,' he said, and wondered why I had not mentioned it. I told him that other doctors had informed me that the pain was a phantom. I was given an inhaler, and in a week noticed a miraculous recovery.

"At the time of surgery, therapists had taught me diaphragmatic breathing. As my chest constriction lessened, I practiced it. It was not easy at first, but I persevered and things became easier, better. I learned more about deep breathing. I found that the most beneficial way for me to breathe was to start from the abdomen, gradually filling my lungs for a slow count of six, holding for six, and exhaling for ten or twelve. There has been no chest pain for more than a year."

"MEMORY HAS BEEN ENHANCED."

A man from a small community in Pennsylvania told us:

"I am in my twenties and have had chronic physical problems for more than a dozen years. I am compulsive by nature and can drive myself into high levels of anxiety. Deep breathing has given me improved control over my levels of anxiety, sometimes eliminating anxiety all but completely. My general anxiety level is much lower now, and I find that I can go further and longer without fatigue.

"I am a dock worker for a parcel service. Deep breathing makes lifting easier, there is less stress on my back. There has been the unexpected fringe benefit of increased ability to think. Memory has been enhanced."

"...RELEASES TENSION IN MY HEAD."

All diseases are a combination of physiological and psychological imbalances, some more physical, some more psychological. In using breath techniques to help heal various conditions, the interface or meeting point between body and mind is explored. "Healthy" doesn't mean just the absence of disease. However effective or ineffective these techniques may be for a given individual, they are intended as adjuncts to normal medical treatment, whether holistic or conventional, which, we repeat, should always be sought.

In Sister Connie Kramer's attempt to manage a chronic sinus problem, she found a great deal of success with the Alternate Nostril Breath technique:

"This technique, rebalancing as it does the left and right brains, reduces tension in my head and sinus passages. I recommend its use to release blocked energy and relieve pressure, which in effect increases relaxation. This is how I was taught to do it:

"With the thumb and index finger of one hand I locate the ridge just under the bone on each side of the nose or nostrils. I lightly press in on the left side as I breathe in on the right side to the count of four. I then close both nostrils lightly with my fingers and count to sixteen. I open the left side or left nostril and let breath out to a count of eight. If I find the 4-16-8 count is too long or even too short to be comfortable, I adjust the pacing to a similar ratio, such as 2-8-4, 3-12-6, or 5-20-10. I find that if I do this a couple of times I am able to rebalance the energy flow quickly and release tension in my head.

"Another simple relaxation technique I like can be used for a quick break during any activity. For this one you just need to put both feet solidly on the floor and then lift both feet, letting only the heels touch the floor, at which time you roll out each foot onto the floor slowly and in a rocking motion. Repeating this simple pattern slows breathing and increases relaxation.

"At times, I imagine my breath as a ray of light that I take into my body and then disperse into every region from my head to my toes. It seems to help to redistribute energy and to relax my body when energy has been drawn to one spot and has begun to cause tension."

"THE STRONGEST AND EASIEST TRANQUILIZER."

"It snowed yesterday. The school where I teach closed early," a woman in New Jersey wrote to us. "This morning, the streets were slushy and slippery and there was mixed precipitation falling. I was looking forward to returning to school today, because I had some special projects I wanted to do. About a mile from school, it happened. A large blue car on the other side of the road came down the hill on a curve, the driver lost control, and the rear end of her car swerved into my lane. I realized I was about to have my first auto accident in more than thirty years of driving. The front of my small car folded up like an accordion and I was pushed over the edge of the road. My first and foremost thought was, 'How do I keep from panicking so I can assess my body and take hold of the situation?' The answer: deep breathing. As other cars stopped and drivers came over to offer aid, I sat in my car (still strapped in by the seat belt) and began taking deep breaths to calm myself so I could deal with the situation logically and sensibly. I concentrated on inhaling peace, calm, stability, while making mental notes as I surveyed my body. My neck felt stiff and tense, but that was about all the damage. Because of the deep breathing techniques and the resultant calming effect, I was able to help the young girl whose car had slid into mine. I held her, offering her support and love, assuring her we were both unhurt. Deep breathing is the strongest and easiest tranquilizer available...all one has to do is use it."

"A GREAT FRIEND AND BENEFACTOR."

In Jane Wright's busy practice as a physical therapist in South Sheffield, Massachusetts, she used control of breath as a method to help her patients withstand pain, both during treatment and at home:

"Pain in the musculoskeletal and connective tissue systems is a major reason why people call on a physical therapist. Muscle or connective tissue imbalance and the physical distortion that ensues can be excruciatingly uncomfortable. Furthermore, many of the various treatment techniques that can assist the body in regaining balance and restoring function stimulate the system intensely and can be uncomfortable for the few minutes of treatment. For these treatments (acupressure, transverse friction massage, trigger-point therapy, facial release) breath control is an integral part of the session.

"Deep, rhythmic breathing through the nostrils assists the patient to withstand pain, and most of all, not to resist it. Fighting or anticipating pain can create the worst kind of pain-filled anxiety on top of the original discomfort. In my experience, breath control makes the difference in these crucial moments of therapy. It is a great friend and benefactor.

"Being sensitive to energy has allowed me to understand another dimension in the use of breath. Physical imbalances or dysfunctions are preceded by energy imbalance in the same area of the body. We all inherently have the ability to perceive those imbalances.

"The vast majority of energy imbalances could be prevented by slow, rhythmic breathing. During an event or situation that could disturb the mind and thus create the energy imbalance, conscious breathing is the only thing I have found to short-circuit this mechanism. By doing this breathing only during an upsetting or crisis time, we literally don't know what we're preventing. My personal experience with the use of breath in daily life and my practice of meditation and yoga are varied and truly wonderful in generating physical health and increased consciousness."

Lots to think about, yes? Time for the I've-Got-Rhythm Breath:

THE I'VE-GOT-RHYTHM BREATH

This breath restores equanimity; do it in any position in which you are comfortable.
1. Inhale through your nose for a silent count of four.
2. Exhale soundlessly for a silent count of four.
3. Continue the breath until you feel recharged.
No one knows you are doing this breath, and it gives you great pleasure and ease.
Nice.

CHAPTER NINE

BREATHING TECHNIQUES EXPANDED

It is in the breathing that God is, or becomes.

—Jewish mystic

Our breathing techniques are designed with adaptability in mind. Most people like to establish their own routines. They start out with three to five applicable to immediate needs. As they become relaxed and find themselves with energy and inspiration, they find other techniques appealing as well.

You will want to invent your own techniques; it is in the very nature of conscious breathing.

The following reprise of our techniques—arranged in alphabetical order—includes expanded pointers. And there's one new breath at the end: Dancing Knees.

ABDOMINAL BREATH:
THE NATURAL BREATH

Best to do in a relaxed setting where you can be alone for at least a few minutes.

1. Lie on your back or stand or sit comfortably and place your hands on your stomach (abdomen).
2. Inhale slowly and deeply, letting your abdomen expand like a balloon. (Your hands on your tummy will feel the abdomen expanding.)
3. Let the abdomen fall as you exhale slowly, releasing old, stale air.
4. Inhale easily. Feel your tummy expand again.
5. Press the air out as you contract, as you pull in your abdomen while exhaling.

Abdominal Breath is the breath we are all born with and many of us lose.

Keeping a hand on your abdomen when you do this breath enhances awareness of the physiological process. Concentrate on keeping your facial muscles relaxed; if they feel relaxed, you will feel relaxed.

Do the Abdominal Breath once or twice a day, for five to ten minutes at a time. Do the breath for a minute or two as part of any Breathing Break. Abdominal Breath feeds into:

PROGRESSION AWARENESS

1. Inhale into your abdomen on the count of 1–2, and up into your chest on the count of 3–4. When you exhale, breathe out of your chest on the 1–2 count and down and out of your abdomen on the 3–4–5–6–7–8 count.
2. To deepen relaxation, sit and do the Ujjai Breath.

Some points of caution:

If you feel lightheaded, stop. When you resume the technique, breathe more slowly and not quite as deeply. Move slowly after ending or you may feel dizzy. Abdominal Breath *plus* Progression Awareness can lower blood pressure. If you are on blood-pressure medication, check your pressure. When it becomes lower—and remains low—ask your physician if he can decrease your medication.

THE ALTERNATE NOSTRIL BREATH

This ancient breath will help you to achieve calmness and clarity.

1. Do a few relaxing Abdominal Breaths in a sitting position and stretch a bit to get in the mood.
2. Close your right nostril with your right thumb and inhale through your left nostril for two counts.
3. Close your left nostril with your right fourth finger and hold your breath for a count of eight. (Both nostrils are now closed.)
4. Open your right nostril and exhale through it for a count of four.
5. Inhale through your open right nostril for a count of two.
6. Close your right nostril and hold your breath for a count of eight.
7. Open your left nostril and exhale through it for a count of four.
8. Repeat Steps 2 through 7 for five to fifteen minutes.

Make your counts slow and consistent. If you feel fidgety, rock slowly back and forth. Use a timer to mark the minutes. (Consult first with your physician if you have a history of heart disease, stroke, or high blood pressure.)

Alternate Nostril breathing becomes easier over time, and ultimately the calm and the clarity you gain will continue through the day. You may even experience lights, colors, or sounds. Don't be alarmed; it is just the natural movement of energies through your body. This breath appears simple, but it is difficult to sustain. The overactive, overstimulated mind rebels against the calming procedure, then shift into a situation of peace. You may feel distracted and fatigued as a result of this inner tension. But stick with it, the rewards will be ample. You will experience a new inner strength and clarity that translates into resolve and calm.

THE BONDING BREATH

The pregnant woman lies on her back; her hands and her husband's are on her abdomen.

1. Perform the Abdominal Breath in unison, with eyes closed.
2. Visualize the baby in position for birth.
3. Visualize the baby's head dropping to engage in the pelvis.
4. Visualize the birth process proceeding smoothly.
5. Think of an affirmation, such as "We now feel the child and ourselves happy and strong."
6. Open your eyes slowly and relax for a few minutes, or longer if you want to.

The breath creates emotional and psychological bonds between parents and child, bonds that can be carried over into the postnatal phase of the baby's life. Many parents invite their other children to join in the Bonding Breath, to feel part of the birthing process.

THE CENTERING BREATH

This breath may be used to create space for yourself, especially in a crowd. Be sure your body is relaxed before Step 2.

1. Perform the Relaxation Breath, allowing your body to relax.
2. Imagine your inner self as a clear light.
3. Imagine your breath pulling you into this inner self.
4. Feel the calmness and peace in this part of yourself.
5. Inhale stability, as if you were a tree growing roots.
6. Exhale fear and anxiety.
7. Look around to see how much more pleasant the environment is.

Use the Centering Breath—it takes only ten to fifteen seconds—when you feel your space is being invaded. If you practice this conscientiously, you will feel centered, not crowded. You will even feel comfortable in a crowd.

THE CLEANSING BREATH

This is a quick stress-discharging technique.
1. Take in a deep breath through your nose.
2. Exhale through your puckered mouth, as if you were blowing out a candle.
3. Repeat Steps 1 and 2 three times.
4. Do a few sighs. Inhale deeply, then sigh again. With each sigh, drop your chin to your chest and droop your shoulders. Think of yourself as a tire letting out all of its air. Think of the tension you are releasing.

The Cleansing Breath releases carbon dioxide from your lungs, lowering acidity and creating relaxation automatically. Think of it as your secret weapon against the challenges of the day.

THE CONTROLLING-PAIN-WITH-IMAGERY BREATH

1. Keep your eyes closed throughout.
2. Begin the Abdominal Breath.
3. Imagine tension leaving your body, like vapor or a stream of color, with each exhalation.
4. Imagine relaxation coming in with each inhalation.
5. Move parts of your body as you breathe, if this helps to release any general tension.
6. Imagine your incoming breath traveling to the area of pain and filling it with calmness.
7. Imagine the pain flowing out with each exhalation.
8. Allow yourself, through crying or sighing, to release any emotion related to the pain.
9. Continue Steps 5 through 8 for five to ten minutes.
10. Feel the movement of your breath again.

11. Stretch your arms and legs.
12. Open your eyes when you feel better.

Practice this technique when you do not have pain; if pain comes, you can easily shift into the relaxation mode.

THE ENJOY-YOUR-MEAL BREATH

This breath is geared toward enhancing the digestive process. Perform while sitting.

1. Execute a few Ha! Breaths to stimulate appetite and the digestive organs before the meal.
2. Do a minute or two of the Abdominal Breath to induce relaxation.
3. Start to eat. As you chew the first mouthful, inhale through your nose for four chews.
4. Hold for four chews. (If you have a history of heart disease, stroke, or very high blood pressure, skip this step.)
5. Exhale for four chews.
6. Do three rounds of Steps 3 through 5 for full chewing of each mouthful. (Be careful not to "inhale" your food as you breathe through your nose. It can ruin digestion as well as cause considerable discomfort.)

Chew slowly so that your breathing is slow. Do this with awareness, so you can taste the substance and texture of the food. Mealtime is a wonderful time to relax. Your digestion (so close to your disposition) will be eased. When you chew slowly, you tend to eat less, which is healthier. Chewing releases tension from the muscles of the jaw, relaxing head, neck, and shoulders.

THE FOCUSING BREATH

For attention and concentration, do this breath sitting, standing, or lying down.

1. Perform the Abdominal Breath two or three times.

2. Imagine yourself inhaling focus and vitality.
3. Imagine exhaling fogginess and tiredness.
4. Feel that you are alone with your task and that all else is superfluous—noise, movements, crowds, thought.
5. Take a deep breath in and out with an audible sigh.
6. Repeat the breath and let your shoulders drop.
7. Imagine performing an activity as smoothly and as perfectly as possible. Concentrate completely.
8. If you are preparing for a race, imagine yourself pulling ahead of the pack at a particular point and crossing the finish line ahead of all other runners. If you are about to go bowling, put yourself into the proper frame of mind by imagining yourself hitting the 1–3 pocket perfectly every time you roll the first ball in a new box. And so on. The image-making technique is a microcosm, a mental stimulation, of the event to be experienced.

Perform this breath as often as you need to focus mental energy. The more you do it, the easier it becomes, the faster it works.

THE HA! BREATH

For total and instant energization. You can be sitting, standing, running, or jumping, but for greatest effectiveness do it standing.

1. Tilt your head up and inhale deeply through your nose.
2. Exhale forcefully through your mouth—issue a loud Ha! sound that originates in your lower abdomen as you bring your head and/or body forward. (You will want to make a quieter or even a silent Ha! sound in situations where barking is not appropriate.)
3. Repeat the Ha! Breath as needed. (If you have a history of heart disease, high blood pressure, or stroke, go easy with this technique; transient rises in blood pressure can occur during Ha!)

A good time for the Ha! is before meals. Allow your body to be loose as you exhale and move forward and down. Because of the Ha!, you will feel more vital and generally healthier. Your digestion will improve because the Ha! tones the digestive organs. Any constipation should lessen as the colon is stimulated.

A good laugh is automatic Ha! breathing. Let's try it. A newspaper got a call from a woman who wanted her husband's name listed in the obituary column—she had found her husband cheating with his blonde assistant. "How long has your husband been dead?" the editor asked. The caller responded, "He starts tomorrow."

THE HIGH-PERFORMANCE BREATH

Do this breath in a standing position for get-up-and-go.
1. Take a few Abdominal Breaths.
2. Snap your right leg up and back in one motion, as you take a Ha! Breath, hitting the heel of your right foot against your right buttock and then letting the foot drop to the floor.
3. Snap your left leg up and back in one motion, as you take a Ha! Breath, hitting the heel against the left buttock and then letting the foot drop to the floor.
4. Repeat Steps 2 and 3 ten to fifteen times.
5. Extend your arms in front of you and make fists with your hands.
6. Pull back the right fist quickly to your chest with a Ha! Breath.
7. Repeat with the left fist.
8. Do alternate pulling, right-left, ten to thirty times, as though you were pulling in a rope.
9. Squat, inhale, hold your breath, then exhale with a Ha! as you leap up with your arms extended.

The movements should be lively and quick on the exhaled Ha! Breath. Make sure you have plenty of space so you can really let loose.

Your movements will become quicker and easier. If your legs and arms wish to move in other directions with the Ha!

Breaths, let them. When you become comfortable with the High-Performance Breath, make the Ha! sound become an exclamation of your vitality. Yell it: HA! HA!

Caution: Be gentle with your movements at first so you don't pull a muscle. If you feel muscles tightening, do the Relaxation Breath immediately to relax them. Don't overdo the repetitions; your body could become fatigued.

CAUTION: *If you have a history of heart disease, high blood pressure, or stroke, we recommend you do not do the High-Performance Breath.*

THE I'VE-GOT-RHYTHM BREATH

This breath restores equanimity, and can be employed in any position in which you are comfortable.
1. Inhale through your nose, silently counting from one to four.
2. Exhale soundlessly, silently counting from one to four.
3. Continue the breath until you feel recharged.

Try matching your breathing with your pulse rate. You should be feeling peaceful. Later, increase exhalation to sixteen beats and inhalation to eight. Longer exhalation creates deeper relaxation.

Use this breath if you are angry or irritable; it will restore you to a calm and relaxed state, and give you great pleasure even if turmoil surrounds you.

THE JOGGING BREATH

For energizing while running.
1. Take two quick inhalations through your nose as you run.
2. Exhale forcefully through your mouth, shouting Ha! (Or it can be a silent Ha!)
3. Breathe alternately through your nostrils, clearing out mucus.
4. Repeat as needed to rejuvenate.

Coordinate breathing and movement. Running should become effortless and enjoyable, and you will be able to run farther. If you find yourself straining, ease into the I've-Got-Rhythm Breath of equal counts: four in, four out, or six in, six out.

THE BREATH OF JOY

This breath helps to pump up low energy or overcome depression or a feeling of low-down that comes over many people midday or after a long lunch.

1. Stand with your arms at your sides, relaxed and in good posture. On a slow, steady inhalation, raise your arms horizontally until they are even with your shoulders; then move your arms in front of you; finally, raise your arms over your head.
2. Hold your breath for a moment.
3. Exhale through your mouth and make the Ha! sound while dropping your head, neck, shoulders, and arms.
4. Repeat Steps 1, 2, and 3 three to five times.

It is best to be loose at the moment of exhalation—feel your grace. Notice your strength as you hold your breath. Notice your joy as you loosen into the exhalation.

You can do this exercise two to three times a day to release any lethargy and sadness.

You will want to create additional movements as you become comfortable with this technique.

You will smile spontaneously—and often.

KAPALABHATI: THE ENERGIZING BREATH

The centuries-old, tried-and-true breath for energy and cleansing.

1. Sit in a comfortable position.
2. Do one or two minutes of the Abdominal Breath and the Relaxation Breath.
3. Inhale fully.

4. Expel short, forceful exhalations through the left nostril while pulling in your abdomen with each exhalation. You will experience a staccato exhalation until your lungs are fully emptied.
5. Repeat full inhalations and staccato exhalations ten times; any inhalation between staccato exhalations should be entirely involuntary and passive.
6. Inhale fully.
7. Exhale fully.
8. Inhale about three-quarters lung capacity and hold it as long as comfortable, then exhale.
9. Repeat Steps 4–8 through the right nostril.
10. Finish by repeating Steps 4–8 simultaneously through both nostrils. (If you have a history of heart disease, high blood pressure, or stroke, don't hold your breath during Kapalabhati. Release it slowly. A person with epilepsy should never deep-breathe rapidly.)

Remember to place a hand on your abdomen to remind yourself to pull it in. Make the exhalations short and strong, stimulating your solar plexus and raising energy and endurance levels. Have a handkerchief at hand; Kapalabhati cleans out lungs, throat, and sinuses. It stimulates elimination and facilitates digestion and assimilation of food.

Do Kapalabhati every day. With practice, you will be able to do it repeatedly. With the consequent ease, you will feel your vitality building day by day. We recommend that you not do Kapalabhati if you have a history of heart disease, high blood pressure, epilepsy, or stroke.

THE LUNG EXPANDER

This breath opens your upper chest area, expanding the lungs. Do it while standing.

1. Spend a few moments doing the Relaxation Breath to open the lungs.
2. Place your fingertips on the top part of your shoulders.

3. Inhale through your nose as you tilt your head back and bring your elbows up, out, and back, fully expanding your chest. (Don't force this stretching motion. You may feel some tension but there should be no pain. Stretching should never be done to the point of deep pain.)
4. Exhale through your mouth, bring your head down, move your elbows forward, down, and in.
5. Repeat this sequence five to ten times, feeling the opening and vitality in the chest. Start slowly, then build up speed as the movement becomes coordinated. Remember to keep fingertips on your shoulders at all times.

If you do the Lung Expander daily, you should be able to work up to twenty to twenty-five breaths and experience a more open and flexible chest area. Breathing will tend to be fuller and deeper, because your lungs will have more room to expand in a more flexible chest cavity. The chest area is related to your heart, or compassion center. You will find your head going back gracefully and your elbows reaching far behind you. The technique creates its own rhythm. The Lung Expander makes you more aware of others' feelings and helps you in day-to-day communications.

THE LUNG STRENGTHENER

Sit comfortably, for optimal breathing and release of chest congestion.
1. Do two to three minutes of the Abdominal Breath.
2. Perform five to ten minutes of the Alternate Nostril Breath.
3. Perform two to three minutes of Ujjai (the Whooshing Breath).
4. Imagine, during Ujjai, your lungs healthy and clear and your bronchial tubes relaxed. See clear, cleansing, and healing light bringing in health with each breath.
5. Affirm: "The stress in my lungs and chest will be released and my breathing will work optimally."
6. Finish with more Alternate Nostril Breaths if you feel like it. Try to see to it that you are not interrupted

during this technique. Perform the Alternate Nostril
Breath for five to ten minutes.

Do the Lung Strengthener when you feel you need to. If
your chest is congested, you may be weaker than usual, so
go easy. The more you do this breath, the easier it becomes
and the clearer your chest will feel.

NOTE: Remain on any medication. When breathing
becomes easier, check with your physician about possible
reduction of medication.

THE PRESSURE-REDUCING BREATH

Helps to keep blood pressure in line through daily practice.
1. Sit in a comfortable position in a quiet place.
2. Relax with a few Abdominal Breaths—four in, eight out.
3. Inhale about two-thirds lung capacity for a count of four.
4. Hold for a count of eight.
5. Exhale for a count of eight.
6. Continue Steps 3 through 5 for five to ten minutes.
   (Inhaling only two-thirds lung capacity will keep this
   breath from unintentionally raising your blood
   pressure during the holding phase.)

THE RELAX-AND-LET-GO BREATH

1. Get in a comfortable sitting position.
2. Do a few head-rolls slowly and gently in a counter-clockwise direction as you breathe deeply.
3. Do a few clockwise head-rolls, also slowly and gently.
   Play at letting go and avoid forcing.
4. Inhale and pull your shoulders up.
5. Hold your breath, hunching your shoulders.
6. Exhale and drop your shoulders.
7. Repeat Steps 4–6 four or five times.
8. Roll your shoulders forward while inhaling
   and exhaling.
9. Roll your shoulders back. Continue inhaling and

exhaling, gracefully, not fast, not slow.
10. Take a deep breath and exhale, making a Ha! sound.
11. Repeat Step 10 three or four times.

Expand your abdomen on inhalation and pull it in on exhalation—in other words, breathe abdominally during the Relax-and-Let-Go Breath. Imagine tension being released from your system as you exhale. Concentrate on your movements. Enjoy the body's grace and harmony. At the top of the head-roll, your head should be far back without straining. Do this whenever you're in the mood. It feels really great to leave tensions behind.

THE RELAXATION BREATH

This breath releases tension from specific body parts. Stand or sit comfortably. Do not move around.
1. Do five to ten Abdominal Breaths.
2. Continue the Abdominal Breath and imagine that with each inhalation you are breathing into a tense or a painful part of your body. (To locate tension accurately, you may need to do neck-rolls, shoulder-shrugs, leg-stretches, buttock-shifts, foot-shakes.)
3. Imagine with each exhalation tension streaming out of your nostrils; the ache you are concentrating on begins to ease.
4. Continue the Abdominal Breath and imaging for a few minutes, or longer as needed.

The Abdominal Breath establishes general relaxation. Use your imagination and the power of fantasy as you breathe out tension.

You can perform the Relaxation Breath two or three times a day for the painful or tense area.

The more you practice this breath, the easier it will be to imagine or visualize your breath flowing in and out of tense or painful areas. This is not an illusion. Imagination actually effects the energy flow. It is capable of directing positive influence of conscious breathing. You will know you have found the essence of this breath when you suddenly realize that it is very enjoyable.

NOTE: Do not overuse the tense or painful area after this technique. There is a natural tendency to do so, because it feels so much better.

THE RISE-AND-SHINE BREATH

Starting the day with this breath should lead to all-day efficiency.
1. Lie on your back in bed. Inhale through your nose and raise your arms perpendicular to the bed.
2. Exhale through your mouth while letting your arms drop.
3. Repeat Steps 1 and 2 slowly six times.
4. Inhale deeply and hold your breath ten or fifteen seconds, or a bit longer if comfortable.
5. Exhale forcefully while pulling your stomach in, then sit up.
6. Inhale and reach for the sky while sitting.
7. Exhale, pulling your hands down to your shoulders and making fists.
8. Repeat Steps 6 and 7 five times.
9. Get out of bed. You're ready for the day. Go for it.

Remember to inhale through your nose and exhale through your mouth. Push your abdomen out on inhalation and bring it in on exhalation. Keep your eyes open throughout the breath.

Some days you may want to incorporate some stretching. Do the stretches you find comfortable.

THE SHIELDING BREATH

Shift from a state of fear and anxiety to one of calm strength.
1. Do thirty to sixty seconds of the Abdominal Breath.
2. Imagine yourself enveloped in a protective white light

as you begin to relax.
3. Inhale the light to bolster the experience.
4. Exhale fears and anxieties. Feel the light washing them away.
5. Surround your space in this white light.

THE STEPPING-OUT BREATH

This breath will improve your posture and revitalize your movement. It is to be done while walking.
1. Inhale for four steps, while walking and expanding your chest.
2. Exhale for eight steps, pulling in your stomach.
3. Allow your back to straighten. Stand tall and proud as you inhale.
4. Imagine, as you exhale, that you feel the tension flowing out of your neck and back.
5. Feel the strength in your step and the rhythm in your arms.
6. Inhale deeply at the end of the walk and let out a sigh, releasing chest tension. You may wish to inhale and sigh several times.

Focus your attention on your back; it will become straighter and more relaxed. You can breathe vigorously and walk briskly. Try not to be distracted by other people during this breath. Enjoy the scenery and the fluidity of your walk.

Ultimately, your walks will be more enjoyable and much more fulfilling in the whole-body sense. As you progress, increase the number of steps for inhalation and exhalation to fit optimal rhythm. Exhaling twice as long as inhaling will have an even more calming effect.

THE STOMACH-PUMP BREATH (ABDOMINAL LIFT)

Do this breath first thing in the morning to help generate bowel movements. It also stimulates appetite and digestive juices.
1. Stand up.
2. Take a deep breath, then exhale all of it.
3. Inhale while raising your arms straight up.
4. Exhale fully while lowering yourself smoothly to the squatting position, hands on knees, head down.
5. Move your abdomen in and out as you complete exhaling, as if it were a pump.
6. Repeat several times, as you feel like it.

The Stomach-Pump Breath, or Abdominal Lift, is an alternative to Kapalabhati. Results are similar.

THE STRESS-DISCHARGING BREATH

Helps you get rid of blah, lifeless feelings.

1. Make sure you will not be disturbed.
2. Get into a comfortable position, lying down or sitting in a favorite chair. Loosen any constricting clothing.
3. Start relaxation with several Abdominal Breaths; breathe in to a count of four, breathe out to a count of eight.
4. Take a deep breath through your nose and hold it. Tense your feet as long as you can.
5. Relax your feet as you exhale with a sigh through your mouth.
6. Take a few deep Abdominal Breaths to the count, as in Step 3.
7. Breathe in deeply through your nose. Hold it. Tense your calves.
8. Relax your calves as you breathe out with a strong exhalation.
9. Repeat the sequence for each area of the body, working from the extremities to the center: feet, calves, thighs, buttocks, abdomen. Next, the upper body: fingers,

forearms, upper arms, shoulders. (Hunch your shoulders up to your ears.) Don't forget your face; it holds much tension. Work it in three stages: Pull your jaw back so your mouth looks funny, scrunch up your nose, furrow your brow.

10. Take a few minutes to relax and let go. (*Warning:* If you have a history of heart disease, high blood pressure, or stroke, consult your physician about this technique. He may suggest a modified version, with little or no breath-holding.)

THE THREE-PART BREATH (CLAVICULAR BREATH)

It's a wonderful all-around technique. Do it anywhere.

1. Inhale and feel your abdomen expanding.
2. Keep breathing in. Feel your chest expand when the lower lung is filled.
3. Breathe into the clavicle area after the chest is filled. Feel your shoulders rising. (You have filled your lungs to the utmost—from abdomen to chest to shoulders.)
4. Exhale and drop your shoulders, relaxing them completely.

Do this breath during work breaks, before exercise, or for rejuvenation if your energy has been sapped. Do it standing, sitting, or while waiting in line. It provides lots of oxygen. (Don't overdo this technique; you could hyperventilate.)

UJJAI

Sometimes called the Whooshing Breath because of the sound it creates. Ujjai means "that which is expressed loudly" or "that which leads to victory."

1. Sit comfortably and loosen any constricting garments—collars, ties, belts, and the like. Make sure your nostrils are clear. Do a few rounds of Kapalabhati. Blow your nose if necessary.
2. Do the Abdominal Breath, but flare your nostrils and

inhale through your nose. Make a whooshing sound at
the back of your throat.

3. Exhale through your nose, making the same whooshing
sound.

4. Repeat Steps 2 and 3 five to ten times.

Ujjai is perfect for deepening the relaxation you have
achieved through abdominal breathing. It creates a stronger
air flow and clears the lungs of impurities. Combine it with
the Abdominal Breath at least once a day, or more often if
you feel like it.

When you do Ujjai, you will become aware of your respiratory system, from flared nostrils to throat and lung expansion. This awareness is the cornerstone of other techniques.
Your enhanced awareness will serve you as a kind of internal teacher, letting you know which part of the body is in
trouble, where to transfer concentration, where to allow
breath to flow next.

THE WAITING (IN LINE) PEACEFULLY BREATH

Take advantage of lines and traffic jams.

1. Do the slow, deep Abdominal Breath with long, relaxed
exhalation. Feel impatience drifting away. (In a high-
way snarl, don't breathe too deeply.)

2. Continue the Abdominal Breath. As your relax, realize
that impatience will not get you to the head of the line
any faster. Impatience only makes the time seem
longer. Einstein was right.

3. See those around you as fellow human beings also
waiting, or working to the best of their ability.

4. Hum or sigh to yourself for a while.

5. Imagine how pleasurable it would be if everyone around
you were also relaxed and trying new ways to be patient and efficient.

Because one gets back what one puts out, you will
discover patience, good humor, and friendliness echoing.

THE WORK-STATION BREATHING BREAK

(Every hour on the hour)

1. Put aside pencils, pens, calculators, and other tools. Turn off the word processor. Put your calls on hold.
2. Uncross your legs and relax in your chair. Sit up straight.
3. Take slow, deep breaths.
4. Allow your abdomen to fill up completely with oxygen. Exhale.
5. Repeat Steps 3 and 4 for a minute or two.
6. Mentally scan your body. Scan slowly from your head to your toes, part by part, area by area. Note the spots that are tense. Focus your breath directly into those spots. You may want to move the affected area if you can: shrug your shoulders, for instance, or move your neck, or wiggle your toes.
7. Feel aches and pains released as you exhale.
8. Experience the areas relaxing and opening as you inhale.
9. Return—relaxed and revitalized—to what you were doing.

In conclusion, let us introduce one more breath:

THE DANCING KNEES BREATH

The name alone revs you up.

Dancing Knees is designed to improve circulation, especially after you have been standing for a long time or have been in a sitting position all day.

1. Do several Abdominal Breaths.
2. Tighten, then release thigh muscles as you breathe deeply.
3. Continue Steps 1 and 2 for one minute.
4. Do a few more Abdominal Breaths.
5. Repeat the thigh contraction-release sequence for fifteen to twenty seconds.
6. Take a few deep breaths, then stand up.

Keep your legs straight—this is important! Your knees will seem to *dance*. Your thigh movement will become smoother, more fluid, and contraction will be stronger. As circulation improves—the object of the Dancing Knees Breath, after all—your legs will feel livelier. And you'll be strengthening and toning your thighs and body.

TEST YOUR BREATHING POWER—
THE ANSWERS

Every answer to the questions on page ix is TRUE. When breath is adjusted, improved, directed:

1. Stress is reduced.   TRUE
2. Weight may be shed.   TRUE
3. Sleep becomes sounder.   TRUE
4. Mood improves.   TRUE
5. Allergies and asthma are
   alleviated.   TRUE
6. Blood pressure is lowered.   TRUE
7. Smoking is given up.   TRUE
8. Sports performances are
   sharper.   TRUE
9. Constipation and headaches
   are relieved.   TRUE
10. Sinuses clear up.   TRUE
11. Sex becomes even more
    enjoyable.   TRUE
12. Appearance improves.   TRUE
13. Work is more efficient,
    communication more
    effective.   TRUE
14. Menstrual cramping is
    overcome.   TRUE
15. Pollution is cleaned out.   TRUE
16. Emotions are harnessed.   TRUE
17. Harmony of body and mind
    is exalted, maximum
    potential is reached.   TRUE

Bonus question:
Breathing enhancements
are as free as the breeze.   TRUE

ENJOY YOUR BREATHING!

CHAPTER TEN

IMPROVING THE AIR AROUND YOU

The Boston Globe, reviewing the original edition of this book, declared, "You'll be better in sports, love-making, and energy in everyday life. . ."

World Tennis magazine described the book as a "jewel… offering chunks of valuable advice…the material is easy to absorb, and the upbeat, positive mood may be just the ticket to success."

"This fantastic book," declared the NBC Today show's fitness expert, and consultant to President Reagan's Council on Physical Fitness and Sports, "is the key to a fit body."

Breathing is in the air. A senior editor at the periodical *American Spa* urges breathing as a smart way to regain energy, naturally: "Deep, abdominal breathing…can relax both the body and mind, leaving you feeling rejuvenated."

"Deep abdominal breathing calms the body," says a professor at Loyola College, in Maryland.

There is a serious campaign throughout the United States to make and have better air.

Better air improves your health, energy, and mood.

A roomful of negative ions can make you feel magically refreshed. Negative ions may be vitamins of the air.

An ion has been defined as an electrically charged atom or group of atoms formed by the loss or gain of one or more electrons, as a cation (positive ion), which is created by electron loss and is attracted to the cathode in electrolysis, or an anion (negative ion), which is created by an electron gain and is attracted to the anode. The valence of an ion is equal to the number of electrons lost or gained and is indicated by a plus sign for cations and a minus sign for anions.

Negative-ion generators are on the market. You can turn them on and they, in turn, will turn you on—and way up. Negative ions help deliver oxygen to cells and tissue.

Negative ions are the ticket. They make the hyperactive calmer. They focus the agitated.

Positive ions, on the other hand, can lead to human distress—aching joints, wheezing, crankiness, apathy, fatigue, depression, moroseness. A barrage of positive ions prompt murder and suicide.

Hot, dry winds—"witches' winds," like the Foehn in Switzerland, the Chinook in the American Rockies, and the Mistral in France—rob us of our good senses, because they spread positive ions. So does air pollution.

It is claimed that negative ions "cure" nothing. But they sure make for better air. They make you feel more upbeat, bubbling. Negative ions pour off plant leaves and falling water. Your bathroom shower is a natural ionizer.

Negative ions have been found to be an effective pain killer. They have been known to tranquilize people in serious pain.

Ionization helps people sensitive to airborne allergens. Negative ions counteract the effects of cigarette smoke. They are therapeutics, because they make it more difficult for germs to grow.

Negative ionization is being introduced into new office buildings. Many buildings, skyscrapers as well as private homes, are supercharged with unhealthy positive ions. Air conditioners strip air of negative ions. Buildings, big and small, don't breathe as they used to. Log cabins breathed!

In 1998, U.S. hotels spent $3.2 *billion* on renovations but paid little attention to air quality. As a result, according to the *Wall Street Journal* (June 18, 1999), "complaints about poor air are on the rise...clinics specializing in travel health say almost 25 percent of patients who are frequent hotel guests now complain about air quality...indeed, many hotel chains admit that indoor air quality deserves a lot more attention."

Yes, let's breathe healthy air outside *and inside.*

Breathe through your nose: It's how ions reach your bloodstream. *That's* where you want the negative ions.

Car exhausts, cigarette smoke, dust, and soot should be avoided; they put a positive charge into ions.

One day, there'll be an ionizer wherever you are.

Plant seedlings have been observed to grow 50 percent more when ion charged. Ionized fruit, we are told, even stays fresh longer.

We must breathe. We have no choice. Plant life helps human life. Plants release the oxygen we breathe. They emit negative ions, absorb gaseous poisons, such as ammonia, benzene, and formaldehyde, and odors. They suppress the growth of funguses and bacteria in the home. They humidify the air inside.

Plants clean, humidify, deodorize, and sanitize the air, inside and outside.

You breathe more than 500 cubic feet of air a day. One cubic foot may contain thousands of airborne particles—chemicals, viruses, and bacteria.

Plants are natural life enhancers. They help revitalize your body every day.

Breathing *can* empower your life.

ABOUT THE AUTHORS

Drs. Loehr and Migdow are popular demonstration-lecturers on breathing techniques for maximizing health, stress management, and peak performance.

JAMES E. LOEHR, ED.D., a licensed psychologist, is president and CEO of LGE Performance Systems, a high-stress training center for athletes and corporate executives, in Orlando, Florida. The author of twelve books, Dr. Loehr has contributed in the arenas of high stress and performance psychology, gaining world-wide recognition. He has worked with hundreds of world-class athletes in a wide diversity of sports. He is a full member of the American Psychological Association, the American College of Sports Medicine, the National Strength and Conditioning Association, and the Association for the Advancement of Applied Sport Psychology.

JEFFREY A. MIGDOW, M.D., a graduate of the University of Illinois Medical Center, in Chicago, has practiced holistic medicine and taught relaxation and breathing techniques for twenty years. He is a well-known speaker and writer on health and stress-reduction topics. He directed a yoga-teaching training course through Open Center in New York City, focusing on breath and yoga to facilitate healing, relaxation, and rejuvenation. He was the principal holistic medical editor for the Time-Life books *The Alternative Advisor* and *Do-It-Yourself Health*. Dr. Migdow was medical director of the Kripalu Center for Yoga and Health, in Lenox, MA., 1980–1990. He is in private practice, in Lenox, MA.

JEROME AGEL, M.S., has written and produced fifty major books. Collaborators have included Marshall McLuhan, Carl Sagan, Herman Kahn, Stanley Kubrick, Isaac Asimov, Buckminster Fuller, Allan Cott, and Humphry Osmond. He is the co-author (with Eugene Boe) of two non-fiction novels, *22 Fires* and *Deliverance in Shanghai*, and he created the computer game *Word of Mouth* and the book and TV series *Thesaurus the Word-Eating Dinosaur*. He originated *Words That Make America Great*, 190 historic U.S. documents, adding a detailed prolog to each.